CONTENTS

PART 4 ☐ POLITICS AND THE PUBLIC SECTOR: RED TAPE, GREEN LIGHT

PART 5 ☐ THE FUTURE OF OUTSOURCING: VIRTUAL VISIONS

ACKNOWLEDGEMENTS

This book was made possible by the endless patience and extraordinary depth of knowledge of its many contributors. I would like to thank the following people, whose invaluable expertise, insight and experience has helped turn this book into a pragmatic view of the often overly complicated world of strategic outsourcing:

Brian Hadfield, Guy Warren, John Smith, Ray Stanton, Peter Armstrong, Jayne Chace, Paul Bevan, Claire Oakley, Stephanie Richards, Ian Ryder, Mike Satchell and Martin Dines at Unisys; Bob Aylott of Orbys Consulting; Simon Shooter and David Strang at Barlow, Lyde, Gilbert; Robert Morgan, Phil Morris and Signe Goldin of Morgan Chambers; Tim Dawes of Nineveh Consulting; Chris Head at Henley Management College; Peter Thomas of UISL; Dave Claridge of KPMG; The Phils, Hickman, Baker and Knibbs from iPSL; Paul Johnson and Rob Watt of ITNet; Ian Green at Dunn and Bradstreet; Demetrius Kofou at EDS; Allan Wall from Symantec; Chris Walters from the Walters Group; Simon Knowles at Computer Sciences Corporation; Jon Kaye of the Belmont Press; Fiona Czerniawska at the Management Consultancies Association; Lynda Morley; Simon Finberg.

Special thanks to Jill Pearcy of Unisys who initiated the entire project.

If I have missed anyone from the list, it is not through a lack of respect for their efforts, only a failing of my own, disordered mind. Thanks to all.

Ian Benn, May 2002

6·99

STRATEGIC OUTSOURCING

EXPLOITING THE SKILLS OF THIRD PARTIES

IAN BENN WITH JILL PEARCY

Hodder & Stoughton

A MEMBER OF THE HODDER HEADLINE GROUP

Orders: please contact Bookpoint Ltd, 130 Milton Park, Abingdon, Oxon OX14 4SB.
Telephone: (44) 01235 827720. Fax: (44) 01235 400454. Lines are open from 9.00–6.00, Monday to Saturday, with a 24-hour message answering service. E-mail address: orders@bookpoint.co.uk

British Library Cataloguing in Publication Data
A catalogue record for this title is available from the British Library

ISBN 0 340 850 507

First published 2002
Impression number   10 9 8 7 6 5 4 3 2 1
Year   2007 2006 2005 2004 2003 2002

Typeset by Servis Filmsetting Ltd, Manchester
Printed in Great Britain for Hodder & Stoughton Educational, a division of Hodder Headline Plc, 338 Euston Road, London NW1 3BH by J.W. Arrowsmith Ltd, Bristol.

M·C·A

MANAGEMENT
CONSULTANCIES
ASSOCIATION

Series Editor: Fiona Czerniawska, Director of MCA Think Tank.

The MCA was formed in 1956 and represents the leading UK-based consulting firms, which currently employ over 25,000 consultants and generate £4.3bn in annual fee income. The UK consulting industry is worth around £8bn, contributing £1bn to the balance of payments.

As well as setting and maintaining standards in the industry, the MCA supports its member firms with a range of services including events, publications, interest groups and public relations. The Association also works with its members to attract the top talent into the industry. The MCA provides advice on the selection and use of management consultants and is the main source of data on the UK market.

FOR MORE INFORMATION PLEASE CONTACT:
Management Consultancies Association
49 Whitehall
London
SW1A 2BX

Tel: 020 7321 3990
Fax: 020 7321 3991

E-mail: mca@mca.org.uk
www.mca.org.uk

CONTENTS

INTRODUCTION

❝ The man who could call a spade a spade should be compelled to use one. It is the only thing he is fit for. ❞ – Oscar Wilde.

For a concept that has had such a huge impact on so many organizations across the world, the term 'outsourcing' is notoriously difficult to pin down. The definition is permanently on the move, with suppliers slicing the market into ever more niches.

Anyone charged with evaluating 'the outsourcing option' will soon find their heads swimming with possibilities: BSP, BPO, ASP, functionally managed services, offshoring, insourcing – and that's just for starters. Further down the road, you will be wrestling with IPR, SLAs, TUPE and a raft of other complex, arcane issues which could mean the difference between success and failure. Is it any wonder so many see responsibility for outsourcing as a poisoned chalice?

It need not be that way. This book will enable you to cut through the mangled management-speak and take a broad, strategic view of the subject. By the time you reach the end, you will be able to:

- ☐ Evaluate your options thoroughly.
- ☐ Select the best route – and the right partner(s) – for your organization.
- ☐ Negotiate effectively and draw up watertight contracts.
- ☐ Implement any changes successfully.
- ☐ Understand and prepare for future trends.
- ☐ Be confident that you've got it right.

Let's start with a streamlined definition, one which strips outsourcing down to its core meaning (rather like outsourcing itself aims to strip organizations down to their core functions):

❝ Outsourcing – allowing a partner to manage a part of your business. ❞

From this initial definition spring several distinct categories – IT outsourcing, business process outsourcing, managed services and business service provision. In fact, there is some disagreement as to whether managed services is a subset of outsourcing or vice versa. For the purposes of this book, this explanation of the difference between the two from Jayne Chace, VP of the public sector division of Unisys in Europe, the Middle East and Asia (EMEA) will be followed:

❝ Outsourcing is a process whereby a company delegates responsibility for implementing a function to a third party. The company retains responsibility for control, strategic planning and integration, but the operations, people, materials and facilities transfer to the outsourcer. In a managed services environment, the client enters a contract with a third party to deliver a service, but the service provider uses its own resources. There is no legal transfer of property or human resources. '

When Abbey Life chose Unisys Insurance Services Limited (UISL) to handle all the administration of its life assurance business (see Part 2, Chapter 17) the company took the outsourcing route. UISL took over the Abbey Life building, equipment and staff and then continued to operate the business on a similar basis. Abbey Life bought the actual deliverable services with contractually agreed service levels in place.

By contrast, a start-up company may pay a third-party service provider to establish a call centre on its behalf. The call centre services may be delivered out of an existing facility that is also used to service other clients. As a start-up there is no infrastructure to replace and therefore there can be no transfer of assets from one organization to the other. So, by this definition, a start-up company cannot outsource anything since it has no assets to transfer out.

This book will explore the different types of, and approaches to, strategic outsourcing. For each, we will look at the pros and cons, examine the risks and the benefits, and lay out tools and checklists to help identify the right approach to partnership.

The book is split into five parts:

☐ Part 1 looks at the background to outsourcing and the broad strategic benefits and risks of various strategies.

☐ Part 2 takes a closer look at the outsourcing market, breaking it down into distinct categories and looking at the drivers behind (and pros and cons of) each approach.

☐ Part 3, 'Practical Outsourcing', is the heart of the book. Here we examine the hands-on issues involved in evaluating and negotiating with suppliers, drawing up contracts, service level agreements and models of governance, and successfully seeing through implementation.

☐ Part 4 examines the wider political and legislative landscape for outsourcing around the world, before focusing specifically on one of the largest and most complex outsourcing markets in the UK – the public sector (including local government, e-government and the military).

☐ Finally, Part 5 explores the future trends in outsourcing, asking how the market is likely to develop.

PART 1

BACKGROUND AND STRATEGY:
A WIDE-ANGLE VIEW

CHAPTER 1

THE BIRTH OF OUTSOURCING

When was the first instance of outsourcing? It is impossible to say – we have been delegating work to third parties at least since God sent Moses down from the top of the Mount Sinai to pass on the Ten Commandments. (As things turned out, Moses threw down the tablets of stone in anger, having discovered just what his people had been up to while he had been mountain-climbing, but as the Bible does not report whether there was a service level agreement in place, the penalties are not clear!)

A more thoroughly documented example of business process outsourcing is the Coca-Cola Corporation. For over 100 years, Coca-Cola has been producing syrup and bottled marketing. The actual production of Coca-Cola is the responsibility of its global network of business partners – the bottling firms. By concentrating on protecting its core formula and brand image, Coca-Cola has managed to build a successful business where the vast majority of the supply chain sits outside its operation.

According to Charles Wang, CEO of software giant Computer Associates, outsourcing entered the vocabulary of CEOs in July 1989. 'In that month, Eastman Kodak Co announced it was stripping away its computer operations, lock, stock and mainframe, and farming them out,' he says.[1] When a global top-50 company undertakes a whole new way of doing business, the world has to listen.

The huge explosion of the outsourcing industry can be attributed to the rise of the concept of 'core competence', popularized by Gary Hamel and C K Pralahad in their 1990 article, 'The Core Competence of the Corporation'.[2] At around the same time, Tom Peters was expounding the need to view corporations 'as Rolodex' – in other words, as a selection of elements, the core parts being handled by the corporation itself, the others being bought in from third-party suppliers or partners.[3]

Hamel and Prahalad argue that by understanding all the elements that enable your company to do business, you can start to analyze which ones provide you with a source of competitive advantage and which can be done by anybody – as long as they are done correctly. Peters puts it even more simply: 'Core competence is the difference between what you do and what you

[1] Charles Wang, *Techno Vision*, McGraw-Hill, 1994.
[2] C K Prahalad and Gary Hamel, 'The Core Competence of the Corporation', originally published in *Harvard Business Review*, 1990; also features in the collection *Competence-Based Competition*, edited by Gary Hamel and Amie Heene, John Wiley & Sons, 1994.
[3] *The Tom Peters Seminar – Crazy Times Call for Crazy Organisations*, Macmillan, 1994.

know.' Non-core activities are those that provide no differentiation, or have no direct effect on the customer's experience – arguably 99 per cent of an organization's activity.

Michael Porter clarified this analysis by describing and explaining the concept of value chains.[4] Today, value chain analysis is a technique familiar to anyone with an MBA or basic marketing qualification: most major organizations have processes in place to analyze their value chains to the finest degree. This 'Lego-ization' of the value chain is a critical element in the success or failure of an outsourcing contract. If it is done correctly, the company understands each step in the path from customer input to customer service delivery, how they interrelate and which are core to competitive differentiation. If an organization then elects to outsource elements of this value chain to a third party, it will succeed as long as the client organization retains responsibility for managing the connections between the Lego blocks and the strategic direction for each element, whether outsourced or internally resourced.

Perhaps the best example of this is Dell Computer Corporation. A little later than Compaq and IBM into the PC business, Dell was among the first to recognize that information technology is an industry built on standards. Industry standard, figured Dell, equals good, and non-standard (even if it is better) equals bad. The company therefore invested a huge amount of effort in persuading the market that the only difference between itself and the market leaders, which were spending vast sums of money on Research and Development (R&D), was the badge on the front of the machine.

Dell had to deal with two other challenges. First, inventory in high-tech businesses goes stale faster than in almost any other non-consumer product business. A processor may halve in value within weeks of coming to market if Intel decides to introduce a faster model in the interim. The same is true for disks and, to an extent, memory. Secondly, the industry has a habit of going from feast to famine and back again with very little notice. Demand can be phenomenally high, or can suddenly dwindle to nothing, depending on macro-economic factors that are just too hard to predict. Dell recognized that in a commoditized, volatile market, the race would not be won by the swift to market but to the company that could:

- ☐ Deliver the best quality – and ensure that everyone would hear about it.
- ☐ Build at the lowest cost (though not necessarily sell at the lowest cost).
- ☐ Manage its inventory and cashflow better that anyone else.

Arguably, Dell is now a logistics company that happens to be in the IT business.

Liam Fahey, says:

> ‘ Talk to any of the execs at Dell – the CFO, the COO, the global VP of sales – and you won't be able to tell which is their role without sneaking a look at their business card. All of Dell's managers understand their customers, their supply chain and their business model. ’ [5]

Dell knows that to deliver effectively, it needs to understand its value chain in great detail. This has allowed the company to identify elements quickly that can best be outsourced, kept in-house or delivered through commercial partners. For instance, the company would never be likely to outsource its sales function, since this is a core competence for the business and starts at the very top, with Michael Dell spending an unusually high proportion of his time engaged directly in the key business of selling.

Dell does not, however, handle its own logistics, preferring to outsource these operations to Walsh Western and Target. Maintenance, considered core by many vendors, is handled

---

[4] Michael Porter, *Competitive Advantage*, first edition The Free Press, 1985; new edition Simon & Schuster, 1998.
[5] Liam Fahey, *Outwitting, Outmaneuvering and Outperforming Competitors*, John Wiley & Sons, 1998.

through business partners Unisys and Getronics, who make a margin on every service call. Both companies also resell Dell equipment, so there is a strong confluence of goals and values between them. Effectively, Dell charges customers upfront for maintenance services, and pays Getronics and Unisys to fix equipment as the need arises. While this leaves a degree of risk in Dell's hands (if it produces an unreliable product it could lose money), it is great for the cashflow – something which Dell manages better than any of its competitors.

The benefits of outsourcing to companies like Dell fall into three categories – strategic, brand-related and financial. According to a 2001 study by Morgan Chambers and *CW360* (the internet arm of *Computer Weekly*),[6] 29 per cent of respondents cite cost savings as their primary motivation for outsourcing, 17 per cent outsource in order to better focus on core business, 13 per cent outsource to improve quality of service and 12 per cent to enable change or improve agility.

This part of the book looks at the benefits and risks of outsourcing. Chapter 2 covers the strategic benefits; Chapter 3 looks at the impact on brand value; Chapter 4 focuses on the financial benefits, both in absolute terms (improvements to efficiency) and in presentation terms (re-engineering your balance sheet). Chapter 5 looks at the potential risks, and finally, Chapter 6 presents an in-depth case study of cheque-processing company iPSL, a textbook example of effective business process outsourcing.

SUMMARY

1   Although people have been delegating work to third parties for most of human history, the concept of outsourcing has exploded in the past decade as management gurus have popularized the idea that organizations should concentrate on their core competencies.

2   By analyzing and understanding its value chain, an organization can focus on the elements that are core to its business and outsource others, while maintaining overall strategic control.

3   PC company Dell has effectively built its business around this idea. It has succeeded by identifying and focusing on key activities such as sales, and outsourcing non-core functions like logistics and maintenance.

4   A particular advantage of this approach is the ability to manage cashflow, but more broadly speaking the benefits are threefold: strategic, financial and brand-related. These will be explored in detail in subsequent chapters, along with the risks of outsourcing.

[6] Morgan Chambers and *CW360*, *Outsourcing in the FTSE 100 – The Definitive Study*, 2001.

CHAPTER 2

STRATEGIC
BENEFITS

The strategic benefits of outsourcing fall into seven specific areas, which will be examined in turn in this chapter:

- ☐ Focus.
- ☐ Quality of service.
- ☐ Recruiting the best.
- ☐ Better technology.
- ☐ Wider skills pool.
- ☐ Agility.
- ☐ Employee benefits.

FOCUS

Since 'core competence' captured the collective imagination of the world's MBAs in the mid-1990s, the corporate world has been obsessed with finding its own core competencies and, by extension, its non-core activities. As discussed in the previous chapter, outsourcing is not a new concept. However, the search for core competence has fuelled its explosion, to a point where the global market for outsourcing is today worth over $200 billion.

Peter Armstrong, VP and managing principal of Unisys EMEA's commercial industry division, says:

> ❝Humans share 99 per cent of their DNA with the chimpanzee – but it's amazing what a difference 1 per cent can make. If you break your organization's value chain down into separate transactions, what, if any, is the 1 per cent element that makes your organization different or better?❞

Most companies proudly boast that 'our biggest asset is our people', yet one of the fastest-growing areas of outsourcing is human resources (HR). Is there a conflict here? Not if you consider HR strategy and HR transactions as separate elements in the mix. The majority of HR activity consists of distributing information about pay and rations, dealing with holidays, sickness and appraisal information, and generating management reports. These administrative functions could be farmed out to a third party with little impact, or better still, automated completely. At the same time, a company lives and dies on its ability to nurture and grow talent, to hire the best and to retain its key people. HR strategy is clearly critical to most modern business.

By breaking the entire business down into transactions, it is possible for management to focus on the points of differentiation and identify prime candidates for outsourcing. Over time, it will be possible to outsource even very small transactions, using emerging internet technologies to weave these separate elements back into the value chain. This concept – called 'standard transactional highways' – is discussed in Chapter 46.

A board meeting is a precious occasion – an opportunity for all of the leaders of the business to gather together, to plan for today and tomorrow. But what percentage of a typical board meeting is spent discussing factors that genuinely drive the business? How much management time is spent on the impact of new employment legislation? requisitions for new IT equipment? management and administration of non-core businesses that are supposed to be cash-cow operations, only maintained because of their low overheads and supposedly self-managing nature? inventory control? manufacturing operations? By contrast, how much time is spent on strategy? discussing customers? evaluating progress against the brand promise? competitive analysis? planning for strategic acquisitions?

Whatever your views on the internet boom, one thing is indisputable: falling technology costs and mass availability of cutting-edge telecoms are lowering the cost of entry to virtually every market. This in turn means that staying ahead demands ever faster innovation – it is no longer enough to do the same stuff ever more efficiently – the future belongs to those who do different stuff. Boards are therefore under increasing pressure to deliver not just efficiencies, but whole new revenue streams. This should come as no surprise; after 20 years of efficiency initiatives (including total quality management (TQM), Six Sigma, supply chain management, enterprise resource planning and, most recently, the optimistically-named customer relationship management) companies are, on the whole, pretty efficient. Granted, all companies could wring a few more percentage points of margin out of its supply chain, and sharpen their ability to manage customer interaction, but in the internet age, the markets are looking for more than incrementalism.

Where does outsourcing fit? By pushing more of the day-to-day functions into the hands of independent specialists, the board frees up brain space to focus on making the core business different – and better.

QUALITY OF SERVICE

One of the greatest challenges in identifying tangible improvements in quality post-outsourcing is that benchmarks are rarely in place prior to the changeover. This is particularly true in the field of IT outsourcing.

As one IT director commented recently, 'I don't need an annual appraisal to tell me whether I am doing a good job – if the e-mail system is up, I'm doing fine, if it's down, I am a failure; everything else pales into insignificance.' One of the biggest problems with delivering IT to a large organization is that of managing expectations. Much as we all moan about flaky software, crashing systems and unreliable technology, the fact is that today's computers are all fairly reliable.

Much has been written about the difference between quality of components and quality of overall service, but the fact remains that we expect our computers to work whenever we sit in front of them. When companies sign an outsourcing contract, they also sign a service level agreement (SLA) to make clear the levels of acceptable reliability. The outsourcing company will be benchmarked against those levels and will be deemed a success or failure accordingly. How many internal IT functions have a similar SLA in place? For the majority, by failing to define standards of service, they are simply being benchmarked against perfection.

Many IT managers claim to have availability targets in place for each operation within their control, but targets by function do not reflect in quality of service for users. For example, if the IT operation has set punishing availability targets – say 99.9 per cent (i.e. the system is up and working 99.9 per cent of the standard working day) for the network, 99 per cent for the servers, 99.9 per cent for the desktop, and 99.8 per cent for each of four core applications – they will be regarded as setting demanding targets for all functions.

Yet from the users' perspective, the system is only working if every step, from their pressing the button to retrieving the answer, is fully operational. And looking more closely at our seemingly demanding availability targets for individual functions, the figures represent a system failure rate of 2 per cent. This sounds good as an abstract figure, but in fact it equates to half a day of downtime a year based on 250 working days per year – frankly unacceptable. Equally important, it also means that there are no availability guarantees for those working beyond the standard seven-and-a-half-hour day. Achieving high availability targets involves a lot of 'planned downtime', i.e. preventative maintenance work on the system as a whole. The system cannot therefore be relied upon outside working hours at the same level of reliability.

The same is true with technical support. Nobody ever calls a support line with joy in their hearts and a feeling of goodwill to all men – my system just crashed dammit, I am in a hurry, I feel stupid and I want someone to sort it out now, or at least accept that it is their job to be shouted at. It is no surprise that the burnout rate in telephone technical support roles is around 18 months!

By setting agreed metrics for both response and fix times, an outsourcer's technical support team can work against clearly understood targets and, in normal circumstances, overachieve against them.

So why don't more internal IT operations set themselves clear metrics and service levels? The fact is, a lot of IT managers feel that by setting themselves up as easy to benchmark, they may be opening the doors to being measured against other providers of the same service. What many fail to realize is that having the benchmarks in place will obviate any need or desire to turn to an outside provider in the first place.

IT outsourcers are used to building their business models around very high levels of service. They cost in the fact that they will have to make early investments in strong, enterprise technology and their return on investment (ROI) models allow them to invest in technology that improves service quality, rather than focusing solely on investing to change functionality, a far greater challenge for in-house IT operations.

RECRUITING THE BEST

Recruitment strategies differ depending on the nature of work being shifted to a third party, but one particularly strong area for generating big HR payback from outsourcing is in IT.

IT staff, more than most professionals, are very aware of CV assets – what is this job going to do for my career? This is driven in part by the pace of change in the sector, which dictates that any IT job is very likely to be a relatively short tenure (not least because of outsourcing and managed service contracts being implemented above the heads of staff). This attitude is reinforced by constant exposure to IT people, either in person or through the media, who have made a lot of money. Everyone in IT dreams of fat stock options and glinting Ferrari.

This career focus manifests itself in two ways. Firstly, IT staff are keen to implement the latest, sexiest technologies (often regardless of their appropriateness to the business need) and secondly, they understand the importance of having the right employers' names on their CVs.

The question of IT staff being attracted, magpie-like, to shiny new technologies has been extensively addressed by Martin Butler, chairman of the Butler Group, in his recent collaborations with Paul Strassman studying the value of IT investments.[1] Butler explored the conflict between the company's will to deliver a project with minimum risk and disruption, and the technologist's will to experiment with new technology.

It is highly likely that the lowest-risk, fastest-delivery approach will be to rely on existing infrastructures and proven skills, to get the project to market at the greatest speed and at its most reliable. Yet from an IT technologist's perspective, the most attractive option is to look to grow his or her skills base and try something altogether more challenging. (Indeed, arbitrating this conflict is a large component of IT operations management.) In an outsourced environment, however, technologists are valued as raw assets. If they have transferable skills or a will to broaden their knowledge, the outsourcer has an interest in nurturing them. Of course, disciplines still need to be in place to ensure the right tools are used for the right job, but an outsourcing company will typically have strong skills development processes available for staff, and is far more likely to have an outlet for those new skills as they mature.

In the hierarchy of great company names for the CV, the major technology suppliers probably top the list – a strong track record inside one of these companies is a short cut to a bigger pay cheque. Attracting a hot technology specialist to work for a sewage farm or a chain of abattoirs is going to be tough, however exciting the job prospects! Equally important, being part of a company that is totally focused on IT presents staff with the opportunity to work on different projects over time to ensure they get a mix of technology exposure. It may not be practical to implement the latest Java-based widget in this project, but there is always another client in the wings crying out for just this type of solution. We will look in more detail at the impact of IT outsourcing on people in Chapters 30 and 31.

In the world of business process outsourcing, there can be an even greater payoff. Imagine that a life and pensions company decides to close off a number of its pension schemes. The dormant pension is administrated and the investment portfolio management continues as before, but the company is no longer accepting new customers. How do the employees feel? They know they are in the dead end of the company. There is no growth or development, and there will be no new initiatives in the future. This is not a natural home for entrepreneurial spirits.

Now imagine that an outsourcing specialist offers to take over this dormant operation and amalgamate it with the closed schemes from a number of other life and pensions companies.

---

[1] Paul A. Strassman, *Transforming IT Costs Into Profits*, Butler Group report, May 2001.

Savings will come from amalgamating administration, consolidating processes and capitalizing on simple economies of scale. From the outsourcer's perspective, the next priority is to sell the service to as many other life and pensions companies as possible – every new client is almost pure upside once the infrastructure is in place.

How do the staff feel in this situation? They are working for a growing division of a major services vendor with a 100 per cent focus on the importance of their role. How difficult will it be to bring talent into this organization?

A personal view

Demetrius Kofou was a 13-year veteran member of the IT department at Xerox when they outsourced the entire operation to EDS in 1993. This ambitious project saw the transfer of virtually every IT operation across Europe on a single day. Only Greece and a couple of Eastern European operations did not switch, primarily because the size of the departments made the change uneconomical.

'I am personally far better off than I would have been had I stayed a part of Xerox. I accept that it wasn't everybody's cup of tea, but it gave me a lot of new chances. I was in the operations group on the IBM mainframe support side and we all did well from the change. The shift managers and operators had a tougher time and many are in the same jobs now as they were in 1993 when the changeover occurred, says Kofou.

The chances I've been given have been tremendous and I've had a lot of very different jobs over the past nine years. I bumped into an ex-colleague from my Xerox operations support days last week and he is now a supervisor running projects in a number of EDS's other accounts as well as Xerox so he's clearly done well too.

A year or so after the changeover, I took the opportunity to move off the mainframe side and into client-server – the hot technology of the time. Soon afterwards, I was asked to handle a Windows migration project (moving from one version of Microsoft's Windows operating system to a later version) for all the Xerox offices in Hong Kong and China. They flew me out there for the three-month project and it went very well indeed – in fact we finished a whole month ahead of schedule. When I got back, I was promoted to a full-time project manager, responsible for all the infrastructure projects in Xerox across the whole of Europe.

The switch from Xerox to EDS was very smooth because EDS told everybody as much as it could, as early as it could. We were kept very well informed whatever the news.

Is EDS willing to promote acquired staff or does it bring in its own management? Kofou says: "Actually, the biggest difference between EDS and Xerox is that EDS is very quick to spot talent. Within a couple of months of taking over the operation, it was picking out individuals for bigger jobs, often in other accounts. This caused some concerns for Xerox early on and the company asked, where possible, for its own people to be kept in the business."

What has changed? "There is inevitably more of a sense of 'them and us' now," he says. "In the old days, we would be asked to do work by other departments within Xerox and would comply if we could. There was no real money changing hands, so there was little pressure. Now everything has to be formalised – new project requests, after all, cost real money now.

EDS is pretty aggressive on the sales side too. Where I see potential for revenue, I am now obliged to push for a sale. It's not really an aspect of the job I enjoy, but I accept it is expected of me and I think I do it pretty well. That said, we still have to tender for some work at Xerox, so I get a pretty good insight into how our competitors work and it is clear that they are all similarly tough about selling.

EDS has been good for me – I've had the chance to try a lot more varied work, seen more of the world and still have plenty of scope for new challenges". ﹚

BETTER TECHNOLOGY

As discussed, outsourcing companies are structured to generate profitability from efficiency, so there is a clear understanding of the importance of using the best technology. At the same time, they are also very aware of the importance of reliability of service – they are usually constrained by punitive SLAs and are therefore under pressure to build extremely resilient infrastructures.

The result is that large IT outsourcers tend to invest heavily in getting the IT infrastructure right first time. IT requirements can be categorized into two groups – functional and non-functional. Functional requirements are those aspects of a system that define 'what it does'. Non-functional requirements address the standard to which the system delivers the functional requirements (i.e. amount of downtime, response times, scalability, ability to handle peaks, recovery time in the event of emergency).

Investments in infrastructure that do not add new functionality are very difficult to cost-justify to the board. 'Spend a million to save two million' is a very hard sell in tough times – perhaps too many reckless promises have been made by IT suppliers in the past for a battle-weary board to accept the argument. For an outsourcing company, by contrast, there is normally a very strong focus on non-functional requirements. Operational efficiency, after all, is an outsourcing service provider's core competency. Consequently, outsourcers focus on architectures, strong enterprise storage infrastructures for power and reliability, and most importantly, formal operating processes.

The market-leading outsourcing companies all have a massive cost advantage over even the largest corporations. Some are the biggest customers of many of the top IT suppliers and therefore have huge control over pricing, terms and even, at times, roadmap. The IT suppliers themselves potentially have an even bigger advantage: as manufacturers of equipment themselves, they can deliver services at a far lower cost than anyone else. In the world of proprietary technology (mainframes and midrange systems), the selling price of the system is predicated not on manufacturing cost (very low), but on development cost. This is the reverse of the commodity PC market. For example, if IBM spends $100 million on a new mainframe processor, it may sell a few thousand systems worldwide before the technology reaches the end of its life and is replaced by a newer, hotter chip. If Intel spends the same $100 million, it will be spread across millions of units sold. IBM's processor development cost per system is therefore three orders of magnitude higher than Intel's. Proprietary vendors fund this investment by building R&D cost into the price of each system sold. While this affects the price of mainframes and midrange systems for the customer, it does not affect the manufacturing cost – in fact, using proprietary technologies can actually be cheaper for the manufacturer than paying other suppliers' licence fees. It therefore enables the big IT suppliers to build technology powerhouses at very low cost.

Finally, unlike IT departments inside large organizations, an outsourcing company is 100 per cent focused on its IT operation. There is a recognition that staff respond well to being given hot technology to work with, and there is a culture of technology refreshment that cannot be sustained inside a corporation where return on investment for IT purchases is measured in fundamentally the same way as for any other form of capital investment.

WIDER SKILLS POOL

The outsourcing market is dominated by the big five companies (EDS, CSC, IBM, Accenture, Unisys) with tens of thousands of staff all focused in the business's area of core competence – delivering the services for which they have taken responsibility from their clients. Unlike a traditional corporation, the outsourcer's HR processes are therefore geared around the staff that enable their delivery capability. Compare this to the amount of focus that a typical organization's HR department puts on staff in an IT operation or cash-cow business unit.

Normally, outsourcers' processes here are very strong. For example, Unisys provides a web-based HR system that enables all staff to manage their own careers – performance tracking, training plans, CV maintenance, development programs for re-skilling and access to all the available internal positions. This creates an environment where individual employees are motivated and equipped to move around the organization. If a member of the team wants to move from one client engagement to another, he or she can track down the opportunities, find out whether there is a skills match, fill the gaps via a development program and apply to move across, all online.

Outsourcing companies rely on this fluidity of staff to ensure they can run at optimum efficiency for all clients – with a smaller headcount when demand is down, but with the ability to ramp up fast as soon as the occasion demands.

In an outsourcing company, therefore, the line between HR as an internal function and HR as a service to be sold to customers is often blurred. Effectively HR becomes a profit centre.

AGILITY

At the time of writing, the world's stock markets are in a period of exceptional volatility. Read any financial publication, and the disparity between the pundits' forecasts is laughable. Building a business based on forecasting the landscape for the immediate, let along long-term, future is no longer realistic. As Malcolm Mitchell, CIO at Vodafone commented last year: 'A good strategy is one that I can get out of quickly.' Instead, management gurus say the key to growth is the ability to move quickly, move out quickly and at minimal cost where required, and to focus the business on its core competence.

Outsourcing operational activity means that a company is freed from the capital considerations, infrastructure complexities and internal vested interests that can so often slow it down.

When recession strikes, companies have to be ready to show a tightly reigned-in cost base and maximum return on capital. Outsourcing can help reshape the balance sheet dramatically (see Chapter 4).

EMPLOYEE BENEFITS

The process of 'being outsourced' is not a pleasant one. From the moment the decision is announced, a number of emotional responses are likely to hit the freshly outsourced employee:

☐ 'I am being "sold" to someone else – I feel like a piece of meat.'

☐ 'My whole world of employment is changing around me and I have absolutely no control over it.'

☐ 'The company I joined and to which I have committed my working life no longer wants me – I feel betrayed.'

☐ 'Who are these new people anyway?'

☐ 'They wouldn't have taken the contract on if they didn't think they could screw more out of us – will I be fired, will I be forced to work twice as hard for the same money, or will I lose out financially?'

☐ 'The things I took for granted were wrong – what else is not as it seemed?'

Yet in talking to outsourced employees, we often hear positive feedback. Why? Despite the uncertainty caused when outsourcing is initiated, there are tangible staff benefits: Remember, if the operation was core to the business, it wouldn't have been outsourced in the first place.

That means staff were almost certainly working in a field that was considered:

☐ A cost centre.

☐ Of little interest to the company and probably poorly resourced.

☐ A management drain (leading to ill-informed, unmotivated staff).

☐ Nothing to be proud of.

☐ Undervalued and underpaid.

An outsourced operation, by contrast, will be:

☐ A profit centre.

☐ At the core of the new company's business.

☐ A management focus, constantly working to keep the staff motivated and operationally efficient.

☐ Proud of its work.

☐ Highly valued, with an SLA in place to ensure the new outsourcers are delivering productive staff and hitting targets.

So, despite their initial negative reactions, outsourced staff are likely to notice many positive differences once they settle down. For a start, their working environment will be more commercially-orientated. While this may be a shock to the system at first, most outsourcers offer training and development to show staff how to stay focused on corporate goals and value their own contribution. Employees will also find that corporate communications are more interesting, relevant and motivational, since these are now geared closely around their particular interests.

But the differences are far from just cultural. The basic corporate infrastructure, such as IT and HR, will also have been designed around staff requirements and aspirations. The outsourcer will invariably have better equipment and facilities than their previous employers, and aims to ensure staff are as productive as possible.

This stems from an acute management understanding that a motivated, productive workforce makes the difference between SLA conformance and disaster. And failing to meet an SLA has three serious implications for an outsourcer. First, the (often substantial) financial penalty; then the fact that the organization is manifestly not reaching operational efficiencies and therefore is not seeing any payback. Finally, failing to meet an SLA could cause irreparable damage to a company's reputation and preclude it from ever winning any further business to balance out its losses on the failing contract.

Outsourced staff therefore work in a motivated, well-equipped environment with a better understanding of the value of their work and a wider portfolio of career opportunities.

SUMMARY

1   By farming out non-core activities to third parties, an organization can free up time and resources to focus on its core competencies.

2   Unlike most internal departments, outsourcers are bound by service level agreements (SLAs). They have a clear incentive to maintain quality of service and can be held to account if they fail. Many internal business units could learn from this.

3   Recruiting the best staff can be difficult for a stale, internal division. But outsourcers offer staff the opportunity to work with a wide range of technologies and clients over time, keeping their CVs up to date. This means they are better able to attract and retain talented staff.

4   In their continual quest for improved efficiency, outsourcers will invest in the best technology infrastructure to service their customers. Economies of scale mean they can offer access to systems that would be beyond the financial reach of in-house departments.

5   The large outsourcers have a huge pool of skilled staff on which to draw. Their HR functions focus on enabling staff to move around the organization, according to their career aspirations.

6   Outsourcing non-core activities frees a company from the capital considerations, infrastructure costs and internal vested interests associated with them. This allows it to be more agile, particularly in uncertain economic times.

7   Outsourced staff gain the benefits of working with like-minded people in a dynamic, commercial environment with better infrastructure, training, support and career development opportunities.

CHAPTER 3

IMPACT ON BRAND VALUE

‹ Nike is leveraging the deep emotional connection that people have with sports and fitness. With Starbucks, we see how coffee has woven itself into the fabric of people's lives, and that's our opportunity to create a frame of mind that's unique. › – Scott Bedbury, CMO of Starbucks, former CMO of Nike

I find this quote slightly chilling. I don't think I want a coffee house to weave itself into the fabric of my life – it sounds too much like *Fatal Attraction* with a twist of decaffeinated latte. Many fortunes have been made in the name of brand expertise. I have seen dozens of erudite and snappy definitions of brand values, but for most large organizations, branding is still perceived as a 'marketing problem'.

For the purpose of this book, let's define brand as 'what people say about you when you're not there'. Your brand is the perception that exists in the minds of your customers and prospects about you and your products. It is driven by two different forces. The first is logic: delivering great service to your customers directly drives brand value; the unique elements of that service mark you out as different from your competition.

The second force is much more difficult to pin down and manipulate – emotion. The good news is that emotional brand strength is long-lasting, and provides scope to grow your business even at times when you are not particularly competitive on price or lack the very latest technology. It is also arguably your most valuable company asset; but the bad news is that it is a fragile thing which, once broken, is very hard to mend.

THE EMOTIONAL BOND

Bedbury is quite right, of course. If the emotional bond is right, customers will look beyond the fact that they are paying $3 for a cardboard cup of coffee (albeit a very tasty one). People are attracted to the ambience of Starbucks, with its oversized sofas and ready supply of newspapers to browse.

Who could have believed that Marks & Spencer would go from being synonymous with quality, to tabloid shorthand for the troubled retail sector, in such a short time? Although the business has recently made significant strides in turning this perception around with the introduction of the popular Per Una brand, it may take a long time for the retailer to regain the special place it once had in shoppers' hearts.

What went wrong? At the end of the 1990s, the company was facing competition from more glamorous brands like Gap and Calvin Klein, not just on cachet, but also on price. Labels became immensely important to the majority of its customer base – especially the most profitable, younger audience. M&S addressed the problem by shifting manufacturing overseas where costs were far lower than in the UK. But this move, entirely logical from a supply chain perspective, proved damaging for the brand and therefore the company's sales figures. The British buying public was treated to bad-news TV pictures of hard-working British employees thrown out after decades of service; of local communities in decline; of picket lines and angry faces. Worse still, irrespective of the reality, British-made products still carry an image of quality in the UK and indeed around the world. Suddenly, one of the fundamental planks of M&S's brand image was in doubt – will the quality still be as good as it used to be?

For Marks and Spencer, a logical decision about its supply chain had an unexpected effect on its brand. Thankfully, through strong product marketing, tight controls and a pretty tough efficiency drive, today the stock price is back up to more than double their September 1999 low. But the lesson is clear – mess with brand values at your peril. By contrast, if the branding is right, there are huge benefits for both your organization and your customers:

For the customer

- ☐ Ability to identify the source of a product or service.
- ☐ Reduced risk.
- ☐ Lower cost of searching for products/services.
- ☐ Promise, bond or pact with the brand owner.
- ☐ Assignment of responsibility to brand owner.

For the brand owner

- ☐ Means of identification and differentiation.
- ☐ Means of legally protecting unique characteristics.
- ☐ Source of competitive advantage.
- ☐ Means of endorsing unique associations.
- ☐ Large intangible asset.

(Source: Ian Ryder, former director of global brand management at Hewlett-Packard.)

As we saw in Chapter 1, deconstructing the value chain enables an organization to understand which elements of its delivery to customers can best be handled by a third party. But get it wrong and the results can be disastrous. Sportswear brand leader Nike was never a manufacturer. From its inception as an import/export company for running shoes made in Japan, the company was never conceived to manufacture anything. Nike's philosophy is clear – customers buy brands, not products. As is thoroughly documented in Naomi Klein's challenging, if at times controversial, book *No Logo*,[1] Nike invested hundreds of millions of dollars (half a billion in 1997 alone) establishing its identification with all that is positive in sports.

[1] Naomi Klein, *No Logo*, Flamingo, 2001.

At the same time, with a strong focus on the efficiency of its supply chain, the company was capitalizing on newly emerging low-cost manufacturing processes. The World Trade Organization was driving developing countries to establish Export Processing Zones (EPZs) – vast industrial estates that could capitalize on lower local labour costs and generous tax incentives. Using them seemed a logical way to fuel further profitable growth. Nike outsourced the entire management of its supply chain to third parties who could choose where to make the products and implement all the management associated with operating factories. This left the company free to concentrate on its core competence – marketing.

All was well for many years, until word started to leak out to Nike's customer base about the working conditions of those actually producing the company's new $100 running shoes. Allegations of sweatshop practices were everywhere. Nike's core customers were treated to pictures of people labouring in awful conditions for a less-than-living wage.

At the time of writing, Nike is well into a vigorous PR campaign to shore up its reputation as a bastion of the principles of fair play. New processes have been rushed in to protect workers from the excesses of the sweatshop (although controversy continues to rage about the extent to which these are enforced). Nike is still, of course, a branding powerhouse, yet the controversy around manufacturing threatened its entire business.

Ian Ryder, former director of global brand management at Hewlett-Packard, has this to say:

> *Never outsource on the basis of pure efficiency – you must take into account the customer experience and ensure that any outsourced activity has, at absolute worst, a neutral effect and, at best, actively enhances your brand.*

INTERNAL CULTURE

Your brand does not just affect your customers; it can also be closely linked to your internal culture. Indeed, companies like Virgin and AIT (a UK-based financial services software house) have actively built their brand around their culture. AIT's Carl Rigby famously goes to great lengths to make the company's culture exciting and compelling. From the grand piano in reception and the part-time jazz pianist who comes in to play it, through providing staff with a $750 interior design budget every time they move office, all the way to hiring a celebrity chef to open the refurbished staff canteen, Rigby's policies show he understands the power of internal culture. Today, recent disclosures about accounting actions have rendered AIT's financial future less than certain, but, as a software producer, their focus on culture certainly helped propel them from start up to exceptional product creators in competition with some of the largest technology powerhouses in the world. Equally, Virgin's success relies heavily on people buying into the relaxed, irreverent, fun-seeking culture it works so hard to build – irrespective of whether they are selling cola or airline tickets, banking services or wedding dresses.

This internal culture drives customer perceptions in all sorts of ways, from 'that looks like fun – I'd like to be involved with that' to the more prosaic 'their staff are really committed – I am sure they will do everything they can to do a great job for me'.

Even if your organization does not consciously use internal culture to drive its brand image, this will happen whether you like it or not. Companies with a culture of cautious incrementalism are unlikely to come across as dynamic innovators, however much the marketing department spends on advertising.

But the impact of outsourcing on your brand can take place at any level. In the UK, Oracle and Microsoft have their corporate head offices next door to one another. Although each has a campus of several, similarly-sized buildings, there is a stark contrast between them: Oracle's huge, central Zen garden versus Microsoft's smooth corporate atrium built around a thriving coffee bar.

Both companies have a staff restaurant and they clearly both outsource their catering. Each has a similar number of food stands, offering a range of nourishments from the healthy to the deep-fried, the traditional to the adventurous. At Microsoft's restaurant, you wander around at your own pace, making choices about what you fancy. Microsoft's brand promises lots of choice – choose the hardware, choose the application, Microsoft keeps your options open.

The last time I ate in Oracle's restaurant, I was struck by the fact that the staff on each stand work *hard* to sell you their dishes – 'try this, its great today', 'this fish is just in, you've got to give it a go'. Oracle's brand is all about getting to the point and getting on with things: do not go out and buy lots of different parts and struggle to glue it all together – we can sell you the lot. Oracle is not ashamed to be a sales company – it revels in it and wants its customers to as well.

Corporate catering as core to your brand? Well maybe. There is no question that your experiences over lunch affect your attitudes to internal and external customers for the rest of the day.

In discussions with potential outsource partners, ask about how they think they can improve the service to your customers, and what positive impact they can have on your brand.

SUMMARY

1 Brand is 'what people say about you when you're not there'. It is driven by both logic and emotion. Be aware that logical business decisions can sometimes have a catastrophic emotional effect on your brand.

2 Conversely, a strong emotional brand will enable you to grow your business even if your logical differentiators in other areas, such as price, are minimal or non-existent (e.g. Starbucks).

3 The negative consequences of outsourcing elements of your value chain on a purely economic basis may take a long time to emerge (e.g. Nike's outsourcing of manufacturing to developing countries).

4 Always assess both the logical and emotional impact on your brand when considering outsourcing any function. At worst, the impact should be neutral. Preferably, it should actively improve your branding.

5 Your internal culture both drives and reflects your brand. You cannot change this overnight. Play to your strengths. Ask potential outsourcing partners how they can have a positive effect on your brand.

CHAPTER 4

FINANCIAL BENEFITS

The number-one stated objective of businesses considering outsourcing is cost savings. However, among providers there is a sense that customers overplay the financial reasons for outsourcing. A recent Australian study of the logistics outsourcing market found that projects initiated purely to save money were the most prone to failure – i.e. most likely to be viewed as unsuccessful by the client.

That said, there are certainly significant financial benefits to be gained from outsourcing and these can be split into six key areas:

- ☐ Economies of scale.
- ☐ Economies of process.
- ☐ 'Outsorcery'.
- ☐ Cashflow.
- ☐ Savings from IT efficiency.
- ☐ Risk-share/gain-share.

ECONOMIES OF SCALE

Particularly in the field of business process outsourcing, the greatest savings come from the fact that the outsourcer is able to achieve economies of scale by offering a similar service to more than one client. For example, administering a dormant pension scheme or processing cheques needs a fixed infrastructure, including management, property, IT and disaster recovery facilities. Widening the service to a second customer will need little or no further management, a modest increase in real estate (certainly not double), a small increase in IT and shared disaster recovery.

In IT outsourcing, many of the giants have built vast, state-of-the-art data centres around the world, which provide a common infrastructure for storage management, disaster recovery, resilience and operational processes. The cost of fulfilling another set of large data-centre requirements is relatively small for them.

ECONOMIES OF PROCESS

'People only outsource problems,' says Claire Oakley, contracts manager at Unisys. Perhaps this is a pessimistic view, but it is true that an organization is unlikely to outsource a thriving business operation which is bringing in new revenue. The typical candidate for outsourcing, whether business function or business process, is usually operated as a cost centre. Turning a cost centre into a profit centre has a massive impact on management disciplines. The management suddenly has the opportunity to split out the work that they do to be helpful, from the work that delivers real value. Non-essential tasks are identified, questioned and either charged out, or more commonly abandoned without any adverse effect.

The liberation in management thinking that comes when an operation moves from cost to profit centre can yield spectacular results. For example, when Unisys took over the operation of Abbey Life's pension schemes, it saw a 25 per cent improvement in efficiency within 12 months (see case study, Chapter 17).

'OUTSORCERY'

This is the magical application of accounting practice to make things better without tangibly changing them at all. Unlike any other form of managed services contract, outsourcing implies the transfer of assets from the client to the service provider. The service provider relies upon the client's skills, critical mass, focus and infrastructure to get a better return on these assets than the client was able to.

When an outsourcing contract is signed, the assets transfer out of the client and onto the outsourcer's books. Even if nothing changes in behaviour or practice, the client will immediately see:

☐ A sale on the books.

☐ A swathe of costly, part-depreciated assets removed from the balance sheet.

☐ A possible reduction in property portfolio, hopefully realising a tidy profit.

☐ A reduction in headcount.

☐ A new monthly charge appearing on the P&L.

For a board whose performance-related bonuses are measured by return on assets or revenue per capita, this is not a difficult decision to make.

There is, of course, a cost to this. The outsourcer has to fund the cost of money over the life of the project and to mitigate risk in taking over these previously unknown resources and assets.

In fact, not all organizations need to capitalize on this type of arrangement. A bank, for example, may see little benefit in what amounts to a leaseback scheme via a service provider – one would hope that a bank would understand and be better able to capitalize on the cost of money than anyone else. In such cases, it may be more appropriate if the outsourcer undertakes all ongoing costs (leases, maintenance costs, etc.), but for the fixed costs to remain with the client. This can work out well for the outsourcer, in that risk and capital cost falls, and for the client, in that the monthly cost can be more tightly reigned in.

CASHFLOW

Outsourcing companies rely on their risk analysis skills and specific knowledge to build models which generate profits over a long period of time – commonly three years or more.

Outsourcers understand that the key to profits is to put in the most efficient infrastructure possible, as early as possible. The outsourcing company therefore puts upfront investment into technology refreshment, consolidation and standardization. It may also capitalize on its immense purchasing power with the major technology suppliers to bring in very high-specification equipment to meet its own IT standards, which are probably far higher than those of the client. For an organization paying for the service on a monthly basis, this means a step change in technology with no upfront cost.

This addresses a common IT paradox. The majority of the IT budget is sunk into operating costs, i.e. keeping old systems operational. Only a small amount of capital budget is freed up to deliver on the newer, more valuable work. But the case can never be made to spend that precious capital budget on improving the operation of systems that support cash-cow or lower-profile businesses. Given that capital spend should be justifiable to investors on the grounds that it improves shareholder value, this is no surprise. It does, however, mean that a company's IT operation is always trapped in throwing good money after bad.

SAVINGS FROM IT EFFICIENCY

As well as the above, it is common for IT outsourcing companies to put together migration strategies for newly acquired data-centres. Initially, the outsourcer usually takes over the running of the existing site, largely using existing resources.

Many of the larger providers, however, have vast data-centres all over the world, where operational processes and technology implementation are absolutely the best. The opportunity to migrate hundreds of smaller, older systems to fewer, larger, more efficient machines in a shared location is hugely appealing. It means lower costs, higher reliability, better return on capital, and a pooling of skills that benefits both the outsourcer and the staff that transfer (if not the staff that do not).

RISK-SHARE/GAIN-SHARE

You do not need a joint venture to establish a risk/reward model. Indeed, it is possible to build all of the benefits of a joint venture into a contract if so required (other than the creation of a separately-valued business unit).

The key to successful gain-/risk-share is effective due diligence on both sides. Unisys's Claire Oakley says, 'The most important skill is the ability to draw lines round things.' She makes it clear that the included and excluded elements of the metrics are the biggest challenge. If risk-share is not tightly defined, either party can move costs between accounting lines to make the figures work how they want. If upsides are not identified and documented in advance, disputes can arise over their inclusion in the model.

For example, in the case of cheque processing, the newly outsourced operation may implement document imaging technology to speed up the process – moving a digital image around the country is vastly more efficient than moving a rectangle of paper. The bank may as a result be able to offer new services to customers in terms of tracking the process of payments, getting more information from branches, etc. Some of these services may be chargeable. So should that extra revenue be included in the gain-share figures?

VAT AND THE UK BANKING INDUSTRY

The UK value added tax (VAT) system works on the principle that from raw material to finished goods, every organization involved in a value chain pays tax on the goods and services it buys and claims it back against everything it sells. In other words, every organization pays tax only on the value it adds.

This works well in most cases, but is thrown out when dealing with VAT-exempt goods and services such as banking and publishing. Banks do not charge VAT on their interest or bank charges; they therefore have no means of recovering VAT on services they procure.

Of course, the banks are paying VAT on their equipment and premises whether outsourced or not, but the big change is people. Once staff are moved off the books, they are being provided as a service and their cost may therefore be subject to VAT.

In the case of IT outsourcing, only 20–30 per cent of the costs will be people costs; the rest will be subject to VAT in any case, so the amount at stake is 20 per cent of 17.5 per cent – a manageable overhead when double-digit savings are being generated. For business process outsourcing, however, people costs are likely to amount to nearer 80 per cent. The taxman could therefore end up taking 14 per cent of the total contract value.

In a typical outsourcing contract, the bank will be looking to save 10–20 per cent on the old way of doing things, say 15 per cent; the outsourcing company may well be looking for a 15 per cent margin, net of cost of risk. If the taxman is taking a further 14 per cent, that means a vast improvement in efficiency is going to be needed to make the service add up.

Typically, outsourced operations were pretty tightly run before they were moved out – after all they have been cost centres for some time and are therefore likely to have been starved of money and resources. Making savings of around 50 per cent is therefore likely to be unrealistic even given the opportunities outlined above.

Resolving the problem

Section 5 of the VAT Act lays out definitions of a financial service. In this section, the exceptions to VAT-able services are also clearly laid out. The challenge is for the outsourcing company to try to match the services provided to the appropriate exempt services in the Act.

Unfortunately, this is an inexact science. Precise matches are impossible so the 'law of best fit' applies – a law which, as the name suggests, is open to interpretation. On one hand, the Inland Revenue has a mandate to collect as much tax as it can for the good of the country. On the other, it has a mandate to protect the consumer of the ultimate services. As a result, there is a thriving, specialist industry built around this issue.

From a client perspective, however, if the supplier cannot deliver the service on a VAT-exempt basis, it is unlikely that you will see the returns you might otherwise hope for.

In the juggling act that an outsourcing implementation inevitably involves, the outsourcer must get agreement in principle with the VAT office before signing the contract, and maintain close links with the Inland Revenue throughout.

SUMMARY

1 There are significant financial advantages to outsourcing, although projects initiated solely for cost-saving reasons are more likely to fail.

2 Economies of scale enable outsourcers to do the job much cheaper than the client company is able, and every new client for a particular service reduces its cost to the outsourcer still further.

3 Economies of process are achieved when cost centres become profit centres, and the consequent liberation of management can yield spectacular results.

4 'Outsorcery' is the seemingly magical use of accounting practices to make things better without changing them in any tangible way.

5 Outsourcers' business models require that they put an efficient infrastructure in place as early as possible. This means that the client achieves a step change in technology with no upfront investment. The client also no longer needs to throw good money after bad to support outmoded systems.

6 Sometimes the outsourcer will shift operations to a well-resourced, shared data-centre which offers further savings in terms of IT efficiency.

7 Successful risk-share/gain-share requires due diligence on both sides. To avoid disputes, your model for both must be tightly defined and agreed upon in advance.

8 In business process outsourcing, unless outsourcers can deliver services on a VAT-exempt basis, you are unlikely to see savings.

CHAPTER 5

THE RISKS

‹An outsourcing contract is for life, not just for Christmas. Getting out of one may be possible, but it's seldom cheap and never easy. As with a marriage, the processes exist for breaking out of the relationship, but it will always be painful. The greatest risk is to underestimate the meaning of forever.› – Bob Aylott, Principal Consultant, Orbys

As we all know, outsourcing doesn't always go smoothly. Most people can rattle off a list of high-profile deals that have gone wrong, and probably even more that we have experienced personally or heard about from colleagues. However, if approached from a position of understanding, it is possible to minimize the dangers. With this in mind, I have identified six key risks commonly associated with outsourcing:

☐ Strategic lock-in.

☐ Integrating the integrators.

☐ Closing the door on differentiation.

☐ Relationship breakdown.

☐ Outsourcers in trouble.

☐ Contractual risks.

STRATEGIC LOCK-IN

Many outsourcing contracts are based on a strategic decision about the shape or operation of a given company. For example, it may be embarking on a program of centralization, decentralization or even re-centralization. An outsourcing deal may be used as a catalyst to make the changes. But putting together a contract on the basis of a business strategy which is impermanent can be very damaging.

Many large organizations looked to centralize financial, IT and other functions during the early-1990s push for rightsizing and optimised efficiency. As harder times bit at the end of the decade, many companies were forced to consider divestment of some of the operating businesses.

For example, retail giant Sears elected to centralize its financial accounting and outsourced the service to Andersen. A few years later, in very different trading conditions and under new management, the company elected to divest of a number of its retail businesses. But divestment entailed building financial functions back into the operating units in question as they clearly had to be self-sufficient. This had an impact on Sears' flexibility, its contract with the outsourcing provider, its speed to market and ultimately its ability to operate the company.

As NTL entered a phase of hyper-growth, the telecoms giant outsourced most of its IT requirements to IBM – both application development and IT infrastructure. Today, NTL is under huge financial pressures and is looking to optimize its operating divisions, yet it is committed to a substantially centralized infrastructure with high monthly outgoings at a time when cash is critical.

Outsourcing can therefore become a major inhibitor to coping with a major directional change. Aylott goes further: 'Outsourcing based on a single strategic model can amount to building in a hidden poison pill should the company need to change direction.'

INTEGRATING THE INTEGRATORS

Many organizations choose to outsource slices of their business functions, especially in IT where there is a vast array of different services – from network service provision to mainframe operation, from desktop services to offshore application development.

These smaller outsourcing decisions are often made at a fairly junior level, occasionally on the whim of a single individual. When major alterations are made to the IT strategy (be they due to business changes or simply discontinuous innovation), the relationships between separate service providers can suddenly change. It is quite straightforward to put in place management processes which connect the separate suppliers, but only if it is done upfront. If you try to implement these processes after conflicts have arisen, you'll usually be too late.

CLOSING THE DOOR ON DIFFERENTIATION

If success in business is all about the magic 1 per cent difference, it is essential that you have control over the elements of your operation that can contribute to that 1 per cent. Understanding where your strategic differentiation lies today is relatively straightforward. Being sure that you know which elements of your business will hold your keys to success in five years' time – or 10 or 20 – is a different matter.

For example, since the abolition of the Gold Standard in 1935, it has not been possible to take a UK banknote into the Bank of England and demand an amount of gold to the value shown on the paper. From that day on, the British banking industry stopped dealing with money and moved into dealing with data about theoretical money. Today, a bank's profits come from its ability to manipulate this information about non-existent money (IT people might call this meta-money). In short, a modern bank is a retailer that uses its merchandising skills to keep data flowing through its IT systems. New revenue streams come from innovations, usually from the product marketing teams that the IT department converts into lines of code.

But could it be that IT staff with strong commercial acumen would be better placed to come up with new products to drive profitability? They may not have the direct customer contact, but who better to understand the *potential* of the bank's delivery capability? After all, we all know the argument that radical business innovation never came out of a focus group! Perhaps, in today's banking hierarchies, this approach is not realistic – but in ten years' time, who knows?

It is not viable to expect an external business-function service provider to deliver you unique, radical product innovation. Best practice? Yes. Economies of scale? Certainly. But uniqueness? Definitely not. It is, after all, homogenization that drives the efficiencies that make outsourcing economical for the providers.

One great risk with outsourcing, therefore, is that it is *very* difficult to go back. Once skills and resources are transferred out of an organization, it can involve years of work to build them back in. Outsourcing increases agility, but at the cost of reducing the breadth of opportunities for radical new product innovation.

RELATIONSHIP BREAKDOWN

In the field of business process outsourcing, it is common for the majority of staff to be engaged in clerical or operational jobs. A few will be driven by career aspirations, but most are motivated by a combination of money and working conditions (flexible hours, shift work, proximity to home, etc.). In many such environments, these people will be represented by one or more trades unions. Union membership protects their rights and gives them a degree of comfort.

An outsourcer has a choice to make when taking over a contract of this nature. Under the TUPE laws in the UK (see Chapter 26), it can choose to take over the collective agreement between the previous employer and the union, or it can serve notice to the union that it operates a non-unionized business.

In the latter case, the outsourcer has to set up a works council on behalf of the newly transferred employees. This option may sound more attractive to the outsourcer, but it may not always be the case. For example, many business processing outsource contracts have been placed by the major retail banks. After years of bitter and often very public wrangling with the unions over branch closures, the last thing a bank needs is the local union representative decrying its vast profits and showing wilful disregard for workers on national television.

Removing the unions from the mix can have at best a detrimental effect on PR, and at worst may lead to a crippling revolt across the rest of the business. Choices about how to work with the unions are therefore critical and can have a far-reaching effect.

If the outsourcing company elects to maintain the relationship with the union, a different type of risk occurs. Outsourcing is complex, with much of this complexity stemming from changes to working practices and contracts. Should the relationship with the union sour during the structuring of these new packages, there is a risk of business disruption, or even all-out strike.

A strike in a newly outsourced business operation can be catastrophic:

☐ The client suffers a complete disruption of service which could in itself be disastrous.

☐ The outsourcer finds itself running a non-profitable contract and is caught between resolving the problem and trying to cut its losses.

☐ The relationship between outsourcer and client can break down as both continue to lose money trying to resolve the problem.

☐ The PR implications for both are awful.

Phil Baker, HR director at iPSL, says:

‹ Unions have come a long way since the dark days of militancy and obstruction. We have worked closely with a number of unions to shape development programs to meet the needs of the newly acquired staff we keep, as well as to do best by those we lose. ›

Working with UNIFI (formerly BIFU, the bankers' union), Unisys developed the Lifelong Learning program for staff joining iPSL (see Chapter 6). This project, initially with the University of East London, has now extended to include universities in Bootle and Northampton. The end of the first year of operation saw the first 12 participants graduating with degrees.

Phil Knibbs, HR partner for outsourcing at Unisys, has the last word:

‹ Partnering with the unions has been a great investment. Our positive relationships are a great comfort to potential customers, who see industrial relations as a major strategic risk to outsourcing. ›

OUTSOURCERS IN TROUBLE

The IT and services industries are volatile. New models such as application service providers (ASP) prove that while a business may sound attractive it is not always scalable or saleable. In the meantime, riding on a wave of hype and enthusiasm, they can destabilise the market for more established vendors. Many dependent ASP customers found they were suddenly reliant on a service with no guarantee of continuity. What if the outsourcing provider crashes?

Once a business process or function is outsourced, it is usually possible to switch to another provider, but rarely possible to bring back in-house. The nature of outsourcing, however, is one of high dependence on the service provider. While it is theoretically possible to switch to another supplier, in practice it can be very complex:

☐ Contracts and terms and conditions need to be agreed, this time in a three-way discussion with the client and both suppliers.

☐ Risk/reward-sharing contracts need to be unpicked to agree what rewards, if any, have been achieved at the point of termination of the contract.

☐ The new service provider has to be willing to buy any transferred assets from the outgoing provider at a mutually acceptable price.

☐ Any new supplier needs to be convinced there is an opportunity to make money out of the contract – it has every right to be sceptical if the incumbent is in trouble.

Often, when an outsourcing contract comes to a natural end, it suits both provider and client to make a fresh arrangement, but where the supplier has hit financial difficulties, objectives may not be mutual. For example, if the client believes the outsourcer is on the point of bankruptcy, it may invoke protection clauses and look to break the contract. The outsourcer will be fighting hard to keep the contract right up to the last minute and is therefore likely to obstruct any handover process – after all, when the business is in trouble, every day that the postman arrives with a cheque is another day of trading. See Chapter 28 for a detailed look at how to protect your business from (or at least minimise the impact of) such occurrences.

CONTRACTUAL RISKS

Clearly, a relationship as complex as outsourcing demands a rigorous approach to contracts, governance and service level agreements. These areas are tackled more fully in Part 3.

SUMMARY

1 Outsourcing has a chequered history, but by being appraised of the risks you are less likely to fall into the traps that have snared the unsuspecting in the past.

2 Take care not to tie yourself in to a strategic approach that may not be appropriate in the future. It will make it very difficult for the organization to change direction if the need arises.

3 Once a function has been outsourced, it is very difficult to bring it back in-house. Beware of closing the door on differentiation. Functions providing real differentiation (e.g. product innovation) should remain in-house.

4 Outsourcers taking over unionized operations have the option to scrap this model in favour of setting up a works council. However, this is not always advisable. It is often wise to keep unions on side, since staff cooperation is vital to the success of most outsourcing deals and a strike is generally disastrous.

5 Choose your outsourcing partner carefully. Are you sure it can deliver what it promises? Is it financially stable? Changing providers is a difficult and time-consuming process, while an outsourcer in financial trouble is likely to obstruct any handover process.

6 Pay rigorous attention to contracts, governance and service level agreements.

CHAPTER 6

CASE STUDY: IPSL

Intelligent Payment Solutions Ltd (iPSL) is the UK's leading cheque-processing company, handling over two-thirds of the UK's cheques. A joint venture between LloydsTSB, Barclays Bank, HSBC and Unisys, it is a textbook example of effective business process outsourcing.

DRIVERS

Cheque processing is clearly the business of a bank – handling money is, after all, what banks do. However, in 2000 UK high-street banks were under considerable pressure. After a run of success for the majors, the market was consolidating and stock-market expectations for profit growth were high. Management time was being increasingly focused on the 'high net worth' customer base – a booming constituency thanks to the strong growth in house prices and the trend in larger organizations towards stock-based incentives for middle and senior managers. Having a track record as early adopters of outsourcing, the banks were searching for further opportunities to strip out costly processes. They were also well aware of the balance-sheet advantages of outsourcing.

The operations team at Lloyds TSB, took a look at the business of cheque processing and approached not just the obvious services vendors but also the competition. They reasoned that cheque processing was a quasi-factory process, with cheques being fed through a range of exotic hardware that sorted, read and dispatched the individual cheques. If more banks were involved, economies of scale were inevitable. They also recognized that cheque processing was a declining business. Further impetus was coming from new Euro legislation. Making existing systems ready to cope with the demands of a second currency meant significant development and capital investment. Adding further partners would surely spread the costs.

Another concern was the threat of further regulation of the industry. The Government was, at the time, talking of setting up Paycom, a cheque-processing watchdog to protect the public against what some politicians dubbed a 'cosy cartel' between the clearing banks. While Paycom seems to have gone away, there is little doubt that some controls will emerge soon. For Lloyds TSB, there had to be a better way.

When Lloyds TSB initially approached HSBC and Barclays, each was concerned with another, similar project – outsourcing the handling of cash. This was another manual process, but with the added challenges of variable quality of notes and huge security issues. Barclays and HSBC set up a joint venture with Securitas. This would leave the banks with both a far higher level of control over the corporate governance of the service provider and the potential to get a fast-growing asset on their books. Could this approach also make sense for cheque processing?

Leading the change

As it transpired, Barclays were ready first. They and Lloyds TSB spoke to a number of potential service provision partners, before selecting Unisys. Phil Hickman, CEO of iPSL, says:

(In the end it came down to culture. Unisys worked on the principle of partnership. Its aim was to build an infrastructure that was designed to run the cheque-processing business at optimum effectiveness, rather than simply service a contract. By setting iPSL up as a separate company, the governance was geared around its own success rather than simply maximising the service revenues for Unisys at every turn.)

What were Unisys's motivations here? A philanthropic IT services company? John Smith, VP of financial services for Unisys EMEA, says:

(We see enormous upside in this business. From the day we submitted our proposal we could see that iPSL could be much more than a cheque-processing service for one or two banks. As the largest cheque processor, we would be uniquely positioned to attract this business from the remaining banks. More importantly, we could see that an infrastructure for processing paper-based transactions could have far wider applications – gift vouchers, airline tickets and so on. We saw iPSL not as a transaction between ourselves and the banks, but as a brand new business venture with vast growth potential.)

THE CHALLENGES

A joint venture sounds like an attractive approach – each party gets something to show for their initiative beyond the satisfaction of a problem solved. Yet the fact remains that 85 per cent of all joint ventures fail – even a twenty-first century marriage has a far higher chance of surviving. Building a viable governance structure depends on a cultural fit among the parties. Smith says, 'Companies do not need to share the same culture, but they do need compatible cultures if a joint venture is to succeed.'

In the end, HSBC's initiatives with Securitas, Merril Lynch and others made joining the initial iPSL consortium too difficult. The company therefore launched with three partners – Unisys, holding 51 per cent, along with Barclays Bank and Lloyds TSB (each with 24.5 per cent).

Clearly, staff who move into joint ventures have to overcome cultural issues, but it is important to recognize that these challenges apply at all levels. The newly created board of directors at iPSL includes representatives from each party as well as two executive directors. Many will have learned their strategic approach from their previous organization. Certainly they will bring with them a set of values, priorities and aspirations that will differ from one another. A stormy boardroom, arguing over differing goals and expectations, will tear up the company as much as similar tensions might tear up a marriage.

Hickman sees a critical part of his role as constantly nurturing the boardroom culture and brokering between the parties representing the parent companies.

(There is a huge amount of risk in a joint venture. Irrespective of the level of due diligence, they are ultimately as leap of faith – especially for founder members. It is not until the business is operational that you can see how well a board can unite behind a vision, a culture and a business,ʼ he says.

THE CHANGE PROCESS

In accordance with EU law (see Chapter 26), staff contracts were changed very little, any amendments made being negotiated in conjunction with the unions (see below). Job descriptions also remained largely unchanged – at least initially. Staff did, however, have all the normal thoughts and emotions associated with such a move:

☐ Powerlessness: 'Something has changed without me having anything to do with the decision.'

☐ Insecurity: 'Inevitably there will be a demand for greater efficiency. That means I will either be forced to work much harder, or my job is at risk. Possibly both.'

☐ Indignation: 'I have been with this company a long time – I had no intention of changing jobs.'

In the processing side of the business the workforce is primarily clerical, engaged in fairly repetitive tasks as each member of staff plays his or her part in the process of turning rectangles of paper into usable data for the bank to process. The majority are second-income earners in their households, and so are unlikely to be willing to relocate. The success of the change program relies not just on new technology platforms, but also the rationalization of the number of processing sites. This too has an inevitable impact on morale.

But productivity was not likely to improve without an improvement in morale. How did iPSL approach this?

The strategy

Cheque processing in a bank is a low-status role. It is widely seen as a dying business and has little investment or support around it. Cheque processing for iPSL, by contrast, is right at the heart of the business. The staff had to understand that in their new position, they would be at the centre of a growing business, not at the dying edge of somebody else's.

Uncertainty is the greatest problem in all change processes. Unisys ensured that – as early as was legally possible within the due diligence process and well before the deal was consummated – a senior management team travelled to every location and spoke to every shift. The management team was equipped to answer questions about their terms and conditions, the company's plans and aspirations, and give an idea of timescales. Phil Baker, iPSL's HR director, says:

ʻWe took the approach of being 100 per cent frank. We told staff warts and all what the opportunities and the threats were going to be over the coming months. Nothing was off the agenda, although inevitably there were questions we truly couldn't answer at this early stage.ʼ

On the day iPSL took over, every member of staff received a goodie-bag containing desk accessories and other knick-knacks. There was a party in each location to reinforce the fact that there had been a fundamental change.

On the same day, every member of staff was given a pack containing information about the new company, the reasons for the changes, the plans for the business, FAQs and details of their own entitlements.

33

For many staff, it was apparent that the facility that they were a part of would be closing down in future. For others, there was clearly an opportunity for real career advancement.

Working with the unions, iPSL signed up with the University of East London (UEL) to put together a Lifelong Learning Scheme whereby staff could apply for IT training. The courses need not be directly relevant to their role, but staff would have to commit effort and some of their own time. In return, they would be given time off for study and course attendance, and access to facilities on site where they could work on their courses. At the end of the courses, staff had to present to a panel of managers what they had learned and how it might apply to improving the business.

At first, it may appear that iPSL gets little return from this scheme. In practice it found:

☐ A short cut to identifying ambitious and talented staff.

☐ Some strong business improvement ideas.

☐ A major improvement in morale – even among those who did not take up the offer.

This highly visible demonstration of commitment to staff helped to impress the message that things had changed for the better.

Working with the unions

Unisys also had to decide whether to make the new operation non-unionized or to embrace existing union agreements.

While walking away from the whole question of industrial relations seemed simplest, the company recognized that the banks were much happier to see their outsourcing partner respecting the unions; they were mindful of the impact that a badly received transfer of employment might have on the rest of their workforce. As negotiations began, Unisys also realized there were benefits in working with the unions. Baker says,

❛ We first approached the unions with a degree of trepidation, but decided to be completely open with them as to our intent. In fact, they made our lives much simpler by giving us a single place to negotiate. ❜

Over time, the relationship has deepened and Unisys now has a partnership agreement in place with UNIFI, to work together to develop the careers of employees and to put together the best support programs for those staff affected by the forthcoming processing centre closures. Today, Unisys works with four major unions and relationships are broadly positive with all.

Growing the partnership – enter HSBC

iPSL started trading in December 2000, and HSBC eventually joined a year later. As the early risks had been taken by Barclays and Lloyds TSB, HSBC accepted that they would have to buy their way into the joint venture, purchasing 5 per cent of the stock from each of the other two banks.

At the time of writing, iPSL has 4000 staff (not bad for a year-old company) and 13 processing sites, plus a 14th for disaster recovery (DR). The plan is to consolidate into six plus a DR site by the end of 2004.

Despite the fact that iPSL has yet to close a facility, the company is already delivering significant cost savings per transaction to every partner, as well as an improvement in independently assessed quality. The efficiencies come from streamlined management and much improved IT.

Now that the company controls 67 per cent of the UK's cheque processing, it should be able to add new clients and diversify. Each partner is very bullish about the potential of the business.

Governance and the SLA

In the case of iPSL, governance is 100 per cent through the board. There is a degree of delegation to the senior management team below the board, but in practice the company operates much as any other independent business.

There is a complex mix of SLAs in place which make iPSL responsible for reimbursing any losses as well as delivering a high standard of service in the face of demanding service penalties. For example, the enormous financial risks in losing a cheque means the agreement is very proscriptive – should they lose a cheque, iPSL is liable for the interest lost on the face value of that cheque until it is found. If it is permanently lost, they must pay the full face value.

So what's the bottom line?

When the initial deal was announced, both Barclays' and Lloyds TSB's shares moved up significantly. Most impressively, in a recent study of outsourcing by Morgan Chambers and *CW360*,[1] iPSL is given a valuation of $2.7 billion – not bad for a company that has only been trading for 12 months!

So, the banks solved the problem of staffing and funding a declining business operation, they have seen operational savings and process quality improvements, they have cut their headcounts by moving staff over to the new company and they each have a significant stake in a valuable new business with vast growth potential.

35

[1] Morgan Chambers and CW360, *Outsourcing in the FTSE 100 – The Definitive Study*, 2001.

PART 2

THE OUTSOURCING EXPLOSION: A BREAKDOWN OF THE BOOM

CHAPTER 7

OUTSOURCING CATALYSTS

Part 1 examined the organizational motivations and strategic drivers for outsourcing. It can be a valuable aid to strategic focus, a means of reducing cost and an opportunity to bring about significant improvements in both a company's culture and its capabilities. But why now? What are the external factors driving the phenomenal growth of outsourcing at this particular point in history?

The explosion is even more remarkable when you consider that, whatever the attractions, there are still considerable emotional barriers to outsourcing – even at the highest echelons of business. Most business leaders still see responsibility for the welfare of their employees as a critical part of their role, even the primary motivator for their careers. While the 1980s saw the rise of bosses with nicknames like 'Chainsaw' (Al Dunlap) and 'Neutron' (Jack Welch), most senior managers would rather not have to reduce headcount.

After the Industrial Revolution, paternalistic magnates such as Titus Salt, George Cadbury and W H Lever built model towns and engaged in social engineering on a vast scale. Those days may have passed, but many business leaders still measure their success (albeit subconsciously) by the size of the estates they survey.

So if management is inherently disposed towards keeping operations in-house, there are clearly other forces at work here. And those external catalysts for outsourcing fall into two broad categories – namely the pace of change in technology and the effects of globalization.

TECHNOLOGICAL CHANGE

In the highly manual operations of the past, there were limited ways in which a service could be delivered. A third party would only operate a similar service in a similar way, but with an added margin on top. However, shifts in the technology landscape are now opening up a host of new ways to deliver services. (In this part of the book, we will look at these specific mechanisms in more detail.) In addition, the sheer pace of change means external vendors will often be in a position to revolutionize old technologies and practices, and capitalize not just on economies of scale, but on economies of skill – reapplying lessons learned elsewhere.

GLOBALIZATION

Globalization has had three key effects on the business landscape:

- ☐ Increased transparency.
- ☐ Wider choice of suppliers.
- ☐ More competition.

Each of these factors warrants further examination.

Increased transparency

A few years ago, it would have seemed unthinkable that a high-profile German business would be allowed to fail by the government and banks. Yet the first quarter of 2002 saw the collapse of two notable German companies – Kirch Media and Philipp Holzmann. In the past, tight relationships between local government, regional banks and major local employers made it difficult for politicians to allow companies to collapse, irrespective of the causes of their troubles. Reporting rules, relative to the US and UK, were much less stringent and it was much easier to handle and resolve difficulties privately.

These days, however, public sector intervention in private companies is widely seen as anti-competitive. (Look at the resistance within the EU to initiatives by the French government to shore up companies such as Bull, in which it holds a minority stake.) In addition, US financial reporting rules are exceptionally stringent and European companies are finding that, to compete for US investment, they are being forced to open up financial data to much more scrutiny. And the trend towards transparency is almost certain to accelerate as highly public accounting scandals such as the Enron collapse add weight to calls for the introduction of more accountable systems and processes.

In this context, outsourcing can be seen as a means to tidy up the balance sheet, increase per-capita revenue and remove ageing equipment that has not yet fully depreciated, even though it may be effectively worthless.

Wider choice of suppliers

The global spread of low-cost telecommunications and IT equipment means that organizations are no longer tied to particular geographical locations: staff can now work from anywhere. One of the early markets to open up behind this trend was call centre outsourcing. By placing a call centre in a low-cost location, savings were easy to generate – particularly if the outsourcer was servicing a number of clients from a single centre with a shared IT infrastructure.

Today, international voice and data communications are reliable, cheap and easy to establish. They also open up opportunities to capitalize on what management consultancy McKinsey calls 'skills arbitrage' (buying whatever skills are required, from anywhere in the world, at any given time). Many large outsourcers are using offshore-based teams to augment their local operations and squeeze ever greater savings from business processes, especially IT. Chapter 10 explores the impact of this 'offshoring' in more detail.

More competition

Globalization has also thrown up new competition from companies that previously focused on different markets. The airline industry has struggled harder than most with this trend, but it is not alone: the financial sector has also undergone heavy consolidation and other industries are close behind. Interestingly, the retail banking sector is probably the least advanced along this track, perhaps because account-holders view changing banks as too much trouble. But even here, governments around the globe are working to loosen the banks' grip over their customers – a signal that no industry can rest on its laurels.

Tougher competition will inevitably lead to a strong focus on the cost of doing business. Most industries now have their own metrics for efficiency. Shareholders measure the effectiveness of management teams on their performance relative to the market (cost per transaction, operating cost per passenger mile, etc.). Here, outsourcers offering a guaranteed price per transaction, or fixed annual costs, have a powerful proposition.

SUMMARY

1 The key external catalysts for outsourcing are the pace of change in technology and globalization.

2 Outsourcers will often be in a position to revolutionize systems and processes. Economies of scale and skill mean they can keep costs down.

3 Globalization means increased transparency, a wider choice of suppliers and more competition.

4 The trend towards transparency is a result of stricter financial reporting worldwide – outsourcing can make the accounts look healthier.

5 Today's global IT/telecoms infrastructure allows organizations to use staff who can be based anywhere.

6 More competition means that organizations need to increase efficiency. Outsourcers offering service-level guarantees have a powerful proposition.

CHAPTER 8

DEFINING CATEGORIES OF OUTSOURCING

Outsourcers bring economies of both scale and skill, but the mix varies widely depending on the area being outsourced. Economies of scale rely on the outsourcer being able to share the service it provides among multiple customers. Moving a team of 100 cleaners from the staff of a hospital onto that of an outsourcer may introduce process improvements and tidy up the books, but there is little opportunity for the outsourcer to capitalize on the pre-existing infrastructure to support other clients.

Equally, there is little economy of skill to be gained if the tasks concerned are already well defined, quantified and are being executed effectively by existing staff. The more complex the task and the further from the client's experience, the greater the value an outsourcer can bring.

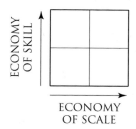

FIGURE 8.1: Four quadrants dividing the outsourcing market

It is therefore useful to break the outsourcing market into four quadrants based upon the type of benefits being applied. The resulting chart (Figure 8.1) resembles a slice of Battenburg cake.

Each quadrant has different characteristics and a different needs profile. Using this model, we can start to plot the types of service we may require and the goals we should expect to meet (Figure 8.2).

Traditionally, outsourcing has focused on business *functions*. In the early days, this typically meant functions that had no bearing on core business – things like cleaning, operating the staff canteen, looking after the office plants, etc. Over time, though, the list of functions suitable for outsourcing has grown to include facilities management, marketing services (but not, one would hope, marketing strategy), HR administration, telesales and, of course, IT.

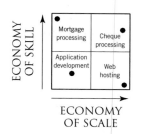

FIGURE 8.2: Services and goals required

But increasingly, the trend in outsourcing has been to broaden out services from pure business functions towards business *operations*. In other words, instead of taking horizontal slices out of your organizations, you take out complete vertical operations. Cheque processing, for example, requires not only operational staff, but also IT, HR and financial resources built into the service.

Services listed in the left-hand quadrants offer better management processes, standardization, business focus improvements and access to a wider pool of specific skills. Those in the right-hand quadrants sacrifice uniqueness for significant economies of scale. Those appearing in the upper quadrants also offer improvements to the way in which a complete service is delivered to the client's end customers, while lower-quadrant services promise benefits in terms of delivering services to internal clients.

TYPES OF OUTSOURCING

We can see more clearly how the types of outsourcing differ by labelling the four quadrants on our chart according to whether the service delivered is a shared or dedicated process, and whether it is aimed at a business or a technical level. Using our Battenburg model (which is loosely based on Gartner Group's model of outsourcing engagement), we can see there are four broad categories of outsourcing (Figure 8.3):

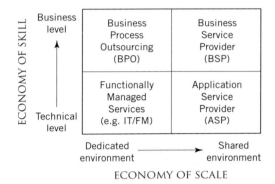

FIGURE 8.3: Battenburg model of outsourcing categories

SUMMARY

1 Different types of outsourcing offer different combinations of economy of scale and economy of skill (Figure 8.2).

2 There is a distinction between outsourced functions (e.g. cleaning) and outsourced processes which may cover several functions (e.g. cheque processing).

3 A service may either be shared by several clients or be dedicated to a single client.

4 In addition, services will either be aimed at a business or technical level.

5 These distinctions are shown in the Battenburg model (Figure 8.3), its four quadrants representing the four broad categories of outsourcing: functionally managed services, business process outsourcing, business service providers and application service providers.

CHAPTER 9

IT OUTSOURCING

IT outsourcing currently dominates the market for functionally managed services (by value). Functionally managed services are those which address business functions as distinct from business processes. They are typically suited to traditional businesses looking to improve their cost base and tidy up their balance sheet. For example, IT, catering and facilities management are all normally operated as business functions that support the rest of the operation, and they tend only to have internal customers. Functionally managed services are delivered as unique packages for each of the outsourcer's clients.

Outsourcing has become the dominant IT strategy for larger organizations. Morgan Chambers and *CW360* estimate that up to half of the UK's IT and telecoms professionals currently work for an outsourcing service provider.[1] Martin Butler, CEO of the Butler Group, talks of in-house IT today as a cottage industry. Few large organizations still invest in huge teams to hand-craft code and build/manage complex systems. Butler expects that over time CIOs will become the true officers of corporate information, devising and operating strategies for capitalizing on the company's knowledge assets. Concerns over the practicalities of IT delivery will be devolved to third parties or more junior staff.

In 13 years of monitoring the hottest issues for IT directors, Meta Group's annual survey has always thrown up the same number-one issue – aligning IT with the business. The sad fact is that nobody has ever successfully demonstrated a correlation between IT spend and business success. Arguably, this should not be an issue – there is no proven correlation between electricity usage and business success either, yet few people doubt the value of voltage!

However, IT outsourcers have built a multi-billion-dollar industry out of presenting a feasible response to this issue in boardrooms across the world. One of the simplest ways is to use effective financial engineering to iron out the big, lump-sum costs associated with maintaining legacy technology through maintenance contracts, upgrades and software re-licensing deals. But in order to absorb such huge costs, contracts have to be very large indeed, and tend to encompass the entire IT operation for periods of ten years or more.

Indeed, everyone in the industry that I have spoken to predicts that it will increasingly be dominated by 'mega-deals' – single outsourcing contracts worth hundreds of millions of dollars apiece.

[1] Morgan Chambers and *CW360*, *Outsourcing in the FTSE 100 – The Definitive Study*, 2001.

Many organizations, however, are choosing to fragment their IT service requirements across multiple partners. For example, it is not uncommon for organizations to have desktop systems managed by one company, development by another and security by a third.

Martin Dines, operations director for Unisys Global Outsourcing, believes the market will continue to be split for the foreseeable future:

> ❢ Clients need to look for providers that can demonstrate that they can work well with other providers. We have been involved in many situations where, even if there was a single outsourcer involved initially, merger and acquisition activity brings multiple suppliers together. ❢

Clearly, competition is alive and well in the outsourcing community.

For many, the concept of spreading risk across multiple vendors – even at the risk of increasing complexity – has significant appeal. The pros and cons of the approach are explored in more detail in Chapter 25.

SUMMARY

1 Functionally managed services address specific internal business functions, such as IT or catering, and are delivered as dedicated services to a single client.

2 IT outsourcing is by far the biggest part of this market, and for large organizations is the dominant strategy.

3 Many believe 'mega-deals' are the way of the future, because only large contracts enable companies to swallow up the huge lump-sum costs involved in maintaining legacy technology.

4 However, many organizations today prefer to use multiple service providers, and see significant advantages in this approach. Organizations taking this route need to ensure their outsourcers are able to cooperate effectively with one another.

CHAPTER 10

OFFSHORING

One of the fastest-growing segments of the IT market is offshoring – shifting development and support of IT systems to third-party teams based in developing countries with a strong graduate workforce.

Although offshore services have been available for many years, it was the Y2K bug-busting scramble that led large, blue-chip organizations to dip their toe in this water for the first time. Local skills shortages forced organizations to venture further afield for staff. Many liked what they found and the market began to explode.

OUR MAN IN CHENNAI, MANILA, PRAGUE . . .

Offshoring is not a true form of outsourcing; staff do not transfer. Instead, the providers offer a managed service, but deliver it from India, Pakistan, the Philippines, Eastern Europe, or other locations with a low-cost skills base. The choice of location is inevitably driven by prioritisation of a set of variables, and both clients and service providers need to balance the following considerations:

- [ ] Time zone differences.
- [ ] English-speaking capability of staff.
- [ ] Political stability of the host country.
- [ ] Host government's support for the industry.
- [ ] Cultural fit.
- [ ] Host country's attitude to copyright and intellectual property.
- [ ] Presence of a substantial, technically qualified talent base.
- [ ] Wage costs.

Russia scores highly on its technically qualified skills pool and its time zone, but the country has yet to prove that it can provide a stable environment for a company to build a substantial, export-focused business free of interference, legal or otherwise. Pakistan is a low-cost area with excellent skills, but its political situation has made it a difficult sell to US corporations following the terrorist attacks on 11 September 2001. China has excellent development skills, but its ambivalent attitude to intellectual property may make developing new applications that provide competitive differentiation seem risky.

In fact, since 11 September, the market has seen a great deal of re-evaluation. Up to that point, India (the bell-wether of the offshoring industry) had seen growth rates of 50 per cent. But now all bets are off, with analysts and commentators split on whether the impact will be positive or negative. On one hand, the new squeeze on IT budgets and demands for faster return on investment is creating demand for low-cost, high-speed development. In this sense, offshoring may be the perfect solution. At the same time, however, new fears about security are driving Western companies to take a more cautious approach, especially to countries perceived as politically unstable (an approach which for many executives can be as much an emotional as a fact-based decision).

THE PROS OF OFFSHORING

☐ Far lower cost: Forrester Research's analysis points to an average saving of 25 per cent on development.

☐ Better resource utilization: if development is taking place in a different time zone, using US/UK-based mainframe systems and networks, the need for expensive upgrades may be delayed considerably. It can also create a 24-hour working day, with specifications being developed during the day and prototypes returned overnight.

☐ A huge, technically capable graduate skills pool: India, for example, has twice as many graduates as the US.

☐ Greater willingness to tackle the boring stuff: persuading European programmers to write thorough documentation is notoriously tough. Western developers, used to capitalizing on their value during a skills shortage, push managers for engagement in the next interesting project, rather than spending weeks writing about what they have already done. Offshore workers do not currently share this attitude, although it may of course emerge in future.

☐ Quality: in response to demand for strong quality standards for software development, the Software Engineering Institute has developed the Capability Maturity Model (CMM) – a benchmark for evaluating software development processes against TQM principles. At the end of 2001, just 14 companies worldwide had achieved the top level (Level 5) certification. Seven of them were based in India.

CONS AND PERCEIVED RISKS

☐ Losing contact with no notice: either through telecommunications problems, political instability or financial collapse.

☐ Language and time zone problems can cause a breakdown in communication.

☐ Security: allowing an invisible third party access to your critical systems.

☐ Too much foreign travel.

☐ Reputation: are you linking your organization with a sweat shop?

☐ Blackmail: what if the company falls into the hands of a hostile third party that is unwilling to release your systems without further cash payments?

Writing in *InformationWeek* (December 2001),[1] Larry Greenemeier highlights the fact that the market still has a long way to go – especially among US companies. He writes:

❛ Although the offshore outsourcing model is gaining acceptance in the business world, it still has far to go to be considered pervasive, even among the largest and most innovative companies, the *InformationWeek* 500. Only 37 per cent of *InformationWeek* 500 sites develop or maintain their applications using offshore service providers. ❜

The article claims that this is not down to a reluctance to outsource – the vast majority already farm out various functions and processes. It also notes that companies with profitable e-business divisions are more likely to ship work offshore (41 per cent) than those without (33 per cent).

Tackling the risks

Writing in *CIO Magazine* (January 2002),[2] Tom Field identifies a series of simple measures to help offset the risks:

☐ Minimize foreign travel.

☐ Keep the code here.

☐ Have a backup plan.

☐ Use a third-party broker.

In practice, there is very little foreign travel required with offshoring. Most offshore service vendors will provide a local team based on your site to handle the liaison. Engagement is therefore confined to progress reviews, which can easily be handled by telephone (or even video) conferencing. It can, however, be valuable to conduct a site visit as a part of the due diligence process. This will enable you to ensure the staff working on your behalf are being properly treated. You will also be in a position to meet key contacts face to face, decide how well you can work with them and form an overall impression of the stability and reliability of the company. It is also well worth checking out its telecommunications facilities and contingency plans in the event of failure.

Field's advice about keeping the code on your own premises is also wise – but perhaps not for the reason you might think. Despite many companies' fears, the intellectual property contained in an organization's applications is probably of very little value to anyone else. Typically, the majority of code is specific to your business, and a large percentage is most likely written to address your own systems' integration challenges. Keeping the code close to home, however, does give you a great deal more control in the event that the service suddenly stops. It also allows you the flexibility to introduce skills from your own organization, or other service providers, should your circumstances change. Internet technology, a plentiful supply of global bandwidth and secure Virtual Private Networks (VPNs) mean there is no reason for code to have to reside elsewhere.

Anyone entering into an offshoring arrangement should also have some kind of escape strategy in case the worst happens. At a technical level, this can be as simple as ensuring the offshore site has alternative telecoms connectivity (Indian telephones, for example, are normally down at least once a day). At a more sophisticated level, it may involve ensuring the

---

[1] Larry Greenemeier, 'Companies Reconsider Offshore Outsourcing', in *InformationWeek*, 10 December 2001.
[2] Tom Field, 'How to Adapt Your Offshore Strategy to an Insecure World' in *CIO Magazine*, 1 January 2002.

provider has staff at your site with access to, and an understanding of, the existing code. Then, should a total shutdown occur, it can take control of the project locally. Those who have truly embraced the offshore concept may even choose to run with a number of offshore partners in different countries.

Field's fourth piece of advice is that, if you are not comfortable taking direct responsibility for this relationship, you can always choose to have the service delivered by a third party. This provides accountability, ease of administration and entirely local liaison, but clearly the cost savings will not be as great – the third party needs to make sufficient margin to cover its infrastructure and risk costs, as well as meeting profitability targets.

In practice, of course, many outsourcers already use offshore development facilities. Accenture, for example, has recently opened two new offshore delivery centres – in Mumbai and Prague – to support its own outsourcing operation. Unusually, however, the company plans to use these facilities for more than just application development. Over time, Accenture intends to add customer relationship management (CRM) and logistics outsourcing services to its offshore portfolio.

COGNIZANT

As a young, US IT company, Cognizant's approach is to place around a quarter of the team on the customer site, with the remainder based in the development centres. The onsite team interacts with the customer to define requirements, review prototypes and manage any changes to the scope of the service. The offshore team handles delivery at the lowest cost. Cognizant's service is built around the common systems that the onsite and offshore teams use to communicate.

This onsite-offshore approach means that Cognizant can work closely with the client during the working day and take advantage of the time zone differences to build a prototype overnight.

So far, the business has shown remarkable growth – in 2001, it appeared in the Deloitte & Touche Fast 500 survey of the fastest-growing US companies for the second year in a row, showing a massive 1039 per cent growth over five years.

One of Cognizant's largest clients is business information specialist Dun & Bradstreet (D&B). The company, which positions itself as a leader in risk management, sales and marketing and supplier management solutions, has a progressive attitude to acquiring IT skills. The relationship with Cognizant began with D&B subsidiary AC Nielsen, a leading consumer market research company. Kim Ross, CIO of Nielsen Media Research, writes on Cognizant's website:

❛ Cognizant has really become an extension of our own IT department, and, as a result, we give more than 90 per cent of our outsourcing work to the company. By working with a third party, we can move into new business areas without diverting the attention of our top developers, reducing our financial risk on such advanced technology initiatives by nearly 50 per cent.

Because Cognizant is such a big contributor to the development, enhancement and maintenance of our software platform – the vehicle of delivery for all of our products – we credit the company for helping us maximize our product revenue, which was more than $500 million in 2000. ❜

Cognizant's relationship with D&B has now broadened to include other areas of the group's activities. What is it like working with them on the ground? One of the D&B software developers in their UK office says:

‹ D&B has developed a module for the SAP software suite that allows automatic, real-time credit checking via the internet as a part of the order acceptance process. Initially the system was developed in Frankfurt, but we now operate a global team. The customer support services are delivered from the US, the development specification is driven from Europe and the US, while coding is handled in Chennai, India. The new team consists of D&B staff in the US, UK and Germany and Cognizant staff in Germany and Chennai. The process of integrating the teams is pretty straightforward – we have had no real cultural problems with Chennai. Occasionally, a mix of poor telephone line quality and differing dialects can mean it's difficult to understand one another but this is readily resolved by confirming all conversations with follow-up e-mails. ›

SUMMARY

1   Offshoring is a form of managed service, delivered from countries where skilled labour is cheaper.

2   Cost savings are the primary benefit, but there are others. They include: better utilization of resources (time zone differences enable 'overnight' working); access to a well-qualified pool of skilled workers, more willing than Western staff to tackle boring work; a consistently high quality of work.

3   Cons and perceived risks include: services going down due to telecoms problems, political instability or financial collapse; language and time zone differences inhibiting communication; data and physical security fears (especially after the terrorist attack on 11 September 2001); fear of unwittingly using 'sweat shop' labour; need for too much overseas travel; systems being held hostage by a hostile third party.

4   Ways to offset these risks include: minimizing foreign travel; keeping your code here; having a backup plan and using a third-party broker.

CHAPTER 11

IT SECURITY OUTSOURCING

One growing trend in an otherwise flat technology sector is the enthusiastic spreading of fearful tales about IT security threats. Trade bodies, user groups, software vendors, firewall makers, consultants and storage manufacturers all have a vested interest in persuading corporations to spend money on solutions that add no extra business value beyond prevention of the ghastly possibility of attack.

Sadly, the doom-mongers have an entirely valid point. Allan Wall, senior security analyst at anti-virus vendor Symantec, talks of the 'democratization of hacking':

❮ Security threats will grow because of an unhappy confluence of conditions. There are more hacking tools than ever before. Currently there are around 30,000 websites worldwide where anyone can go to download specialist hacking tools.

The drive towards internet-enabled business is opening up more and more organizations to the outside world. In a typical e-business architecture, there are connections on the supply side of the system linking into suppliers' and partners' systems, connections on the sell side linking in to exchanges and customers. In many cases there are also links to specialist service providers within the supply chain such as D&B's credit-checking facilities. The web is growing all the time so there are more sites and therefore more entry points into the network.

Military and terrorist conflicts also tend to spill over into the internet, with some countries drawing much of the fire. Being a US company can be enough to render an organization a 'legitimate' target to some, and a recent report from e-commerce risk management specialist Mi2g suggests that 42 per cent of web defacements in the Middle East over the last three years have been to Israeli websites.

Both anti-capitalist and anti-state activism is growing at the moment, primarily among a community of technically literate young people with plenty of access to technology. Human nature is the one constant – people can still be disgruntled, vindictive, inflamed or just plain mischievous. In other words, the opportunity is increasing, the population *with* the opportunity is growing, and the percentage of that population with the will to do damage is probably about constant. ❯

Ray Stanton, director of the Security Centre of Excellence at Unisys, believes IT security is in itself a misleading term:

> (The task encompasses IT security, physically securing sites, disaster recovery, contingency planning, behavioural change and a lot more. I would prefer to call it business protection.)

While I take his point, I think business protection is too vague a term and have chosen to stick with IT security – it may oversimplify but it is widely recognized.

Implementing IT security is always going to be made more difficult by the fact that the target is always at a strategic disadvantage to the aggressor. Security industry developers and potential victims can only second-guess possible modes of attack or respond to actual incidents. Either way, the bad guys have the advantage. To make matters even more challenging, new thinking in the developer community informs all programmers, whatever their intentions. For example, most modern developers are familiar with the concept of reusing code. In other words, rather than writing every application from scratch, they will look to string together the 'best bits' of existing viruses, worms and Trojan horses to build incredibly powerful new threats that are, each time, massively more sophisticated than their predecessors.

As well as the basics of malign forces attacking from outside, there are also two other considerations – data protection and disaster recovery:

☐ The UK's Data Protection Act states that companies are responsible for ensuring any data they hold on an individual is correct, up to date, available to the individual and only held for as long as it is needed. There is also an obligation of confidentiality. This is similar to legislation in most other Western countries and less stringent than many. There is a clear security implication here – if there is a leak, the company can be prosecuted.

☐ Disasters resulting in significant loss of data usually have terminal consequences for companies within five years. Major international incidents always have a temporary impact on disaster recovery provisioning, as companies recognize that the unthinkable could happen to them. However, these anxieties pass, and with them the will to invest in non-functional technologies (i.e. those which do not enhance the way in which day-to-day business is carried out).

PROTECTING THE BUSINESS

There is no perfect solution to security, but there is at least a form of protection against class actions from shareholders following an incident (which could arise if there is suspicion or evidence of negligence). A code of best practice for information security has been defined by the British Standards Institute and enshrined in the new standard, BS7799. This encompasses not just software-based security, but also disaster recovery, backup/restore strategies and physical security. There are two parts to the standard – the first is a directive while the second defines specific processes that must be followed. Companies can therefore be certified to a BS7799 Part 2 standard. Most other countries have now created their own local standards based, to a greater or lesser extent upon the British one. AS4444 (Australia) and NZ4444 (New Zealand), for example, are identical to BS7799.

The International Standards Organization has also adopted the BS standard under a new global code of practice – ISO17799. This gives a single world standard and removes the inevitable political difficulties of asking companies in one country to conform to a standard invented elsewhere. (ISO17799 does not, however, include specific processes and organizations cannot therefore be certified.)

Arguably, not only will companies that apply the ISO17799 standard have a much lower exposure to successful attacks, but they will also have a credible defence to their shareholders should the need arise: 'We weren't negligent – we fully embraced the ISO17799 standard and therefore did everything that could be expected of us.'

IT SECURITY – WHOSE JOB?

Herein lies the challenge. Existing IT operational staff cannot be expected or relied upon to take on the role of policeman, enforcer or corporate guardian. For a start, the person responsible has to report right to the top of the company if the role is to have any value at all. The auditors can not be expected to take it on either, because that would compromise their independence when they report on the client's compliance. The IT director has other considerations and, given the competing pressures of prudence and speed of delivery, cannot always carry out both jobs satisfactorily.

There is also a demographic issue in IT departments. The first generation of IT staff, trained in data-centre practices and mainframe dynamics, were acutely conscious of the need for security as a confluence of technology and process. Windows- and internet-generation technicians tend to think of security purely in the context of software functionality – if the data is encrypted, the system is secure. Stanton gives an example:

‹ A system is built with an effective intrusion detection system. This can track hacks and notify the administrator when an unauthorized individual attempts to log into the system. That's great, but then what? What do you do with the information? What is the incident management policy? Who needs to be involved? How do we involve them? What do we do next? The problem with security incidents is that they require very far-reaching responses. It would not be unreasonable to expect to see HR, legal, executive and departmental management staff and unions involved in deciding on and implementing a response, alongside IT people and the security team. ›

Companies are therefore faced with creating a whole new infrastructure dedicated to IT security. For a large company, this will not be a small team either. As IT security pundits often say, you are only as good as your last update. In other words, there is a never-ending task to ensure that all defences are up-to-date and working. The team has to keep up with all the latest threats, judging what response is needed. The security team also has to liaise with every division of the company and at every level.

At the same time, new IT developments can often lead to apparent conflicts in policy which the security team must work through without appreciably slowing down project development time. For example, a new project may be specified by developers who select new technologies that the security team may not have cleared for use. Security experts are very cautious about approving new software versions without rigorous testing and research. Software suppliers such as Microsoft have, after all, had a woeful track record in delivering secure new products, to the extent that in 2002 Bill Gates has had to make a public commitment to refocusing development on security.

For many there is only one ready solution – hand the implementation of security measures to a third party.

THE OUTSOURCING OF SECURITY

Outsourcing security will normally have to start with a business case. In a traditional IT business case, the primary metric is return on investment (ROI). If we invest X, we should expect to see a financial return of X+.

Clearly ROI models do not work when trying to place a value on security, so how do we approach the problem? IT security investments are akin to spending money on insurance policies. A few years ago, one of the major British retail chains decided to stop insuring its stores against a fire breaking out after trading hours. It found it was cheaper to invest in effective prevention and absorb the cost of the few instances of damage itself, rather than see the regular outflow of insurance premiums.

Just as the retailer made risk calculations, IT operations have to take the same approach to calculating the risks associated with data security. There are three factors to consider:

☐ What is the maximum cost to the business should an attack or disaster occur?

☐ What is the cost of prevention?

☐ What does the company have to do as a minimum to ensure that it is not open to the charge of negligence in the event of an incident?

Weighing these factors should enable the enterprise to make decisions about its security strategy and any outsourcing budget.

The exception is new internet projects. Here effective security can be costed into the overall ROI calculations. Plans for a new banking service will clearly need to ensure both the integrity of the service and protection of the bank's reputation.

The next question to ask is, which supplier you should rely on. Allan Wall believes the considerations, in order, are:

☐ Can we trust them absolutely?

☐ Are they competent?

☐ Can they cover the geographical areas we need them to with consistent capability?

Another dimension of IT security, especially in internet-based industries, is brand value. Retailer Marks & Spencer is famous for its no-questions-asked returns policy. Despite the huge cost of this proposition, the promise that customers can bring things back if they are not happy drives an enormous level of brand trust. By contrast, imagine an internet bank that let customers down through poor security implementation. An effective security program can be used to increase trust in the brand. At that point, security becomes an enabler rather than just an insurance policy.

Guarding the doors

Many organizations build very strong security policies around their sell-side systems. Ray Stanton at Unisys says:

❝ Why should companies worry so much about a heavily protected 2Mb pipe to the internet when they also have literally hundreds of other, less well-controlled links to suppliers and partners? Outsourcing providers will usually want to standardize and rationalize the links so they can be properly monitored. Curiously, most companies won't do this if they are handling security in-house because it is seen as too expensive. A couple of years ago I was involved in a project to do just this for a large defence contractor. We found 70 unused internet links. Apart from the security implications, turning them off saved the company £200,000 a quarter in telecoms standing charges. ᠈

Outsourcing security – the metrics

IT security effectiveness falls into three basic categories, conveniently spelling out the acronym CIA:

Confidentiality – keeping information visible only to the right people. This includes such areas as prevention of misuse of privileged accounts by internal or external users.

Integrity – keeping the data true and accurate. This includes defacement of websites as well as data tampering.

Availability – keeping the system working in the face of hostile attack. This includes prevention or resolution of virus/worm/Trojan horse attacks or denial of service attacks (where an organization's systems are overwhelmed by a huge volume of hits, specifically designed to bring them to a halt).

Although the security experts may refer to CIA, in practice, business heads tend to be interested almost exclusively in the 'A' – 'if the system isn't available, I am not trading'. Persuading bosses to be interested in confidentiality and integrity is far more difficult.

The problem with translating these concepts into service levels is that a breach can remain undetected and is therefore impossible to measure. If an outsourcer is being paid to detect instances of unauthorized access to confidential information, how will anyone know if it fails to spot one?

According to Wall, the best solution is to build the metrics not around results, but around the effective implementation of BS7799. You cannot measure an outsourcer on the basis of whether data is inappropriately accessed, but it is entirely reasonable to measure the time it takes the outsourcer to notify you when such a breach is detected.

Most large organizations now appoint third parties to audit them for conformance to ISO9000 – the global quality standard. It is a good idea to consider taking the same approach with a security outsourcer, ensuring a third party assesses the supplier's conformance and identifies any weaknesses.

ASP or functionally managed service?

Most of the action in IT security takes place on the edge of a company's network – either inwards with virus attacks, hacking or snooping, or outwards with staff sending racist, confidential or pornographic material, or accessing inappropriate material over the internet.

Policing the borders is entirely practical on a remote basis. A service provider with the right tools and access rights can monitor an organization very effectively. Such services carry all the benefits of the ASP cost model – the vendor is selling the same service to many clients and can therefore charge much less than a tailored service or an in-house team (see Chapter 15). There is a further benefit: it is far easier to disengage and reappoint another provider than with a service sharing staff and resources.

In larger organizations, however, there is another security threat – internal breaches. An external service polices only the effective implementation of rules pertaining to the

55

company's external communications. An internal outsourcing engagement requires a higher degree of integration of both technology and staff. You need to address complex issues of access rights to corporate data. At this point, an ASP model is no longer viable and a more traditional, functionally managed approach is demanded.

The other great challenge with ASPs is that most deliver their services exclusively via the internet – which many people think makes it impossible for them to guarantee quality of service. There is a consensus among security experts I have met that one day the entire internet will be brought down by a sustained denial of service attack. I am sure some security experts think they see hackers in every corner, just as some off-duty policemen suspect everyone they meet is a criminal, but this does not mean the risk is non-existent.

A number of companies are looking to break into IT security outsourcing, from anti-virus software vendors (10 per cent of Symantec's $1.2 billion revenues already come from IT services), through diversifying PC dealers to the top outsourcers like EDS and CSC. The case for outsourcing security is evidently strong, but why would a company go to a specialist security outsourcer if they already have their IT operation outsourced to a third party? According to Ray Stanton, it comes down to the core competence of the outsourcer. If a company has a nerve centre tracking the latest developments, trends and attacks and links into the firewall, software and networking vendors to fix problems fixed quickly, it will have a significant lead on a generalist IT services provider.

At this early stage in the market, specialist companies clearly have more expertise and a fuller portfolio of services, but over time it is likely that IT security will become just one more facet of the fully managed services offered by the big outsourcers.

SUMMARY

1 Fearful tales of IT security threats abound, but there is real reason for concern. Ever more people have access to the knowledge, tools and motivation to attack systems.

2 Viruses, Worms and Trojan Horses are becoming increasingly more sophisticated and damaging.

3 As well as external threats, companies also need to comply with data protection legislation and ensure effective disaster recovery procedures are in place.

4 Compliance with security standards such as BS7799 or ISO17799 greatly lowers an organization's exposure to risk as well as giving it a sound defence against accusations of negligence.

5 Security needs to be a key consideration right across the organization, at all levels. This generally either means the creation of an extensive, well-staffed internal security infrastructure, or outsourcing.

6 Investment in security cannot usually be justified in traditional ROI terms. It is more like insurance and should be based on sound risk assessment. The exception is internet companies, where security (or lack of it) can have a direct impact on service and brand (e.g. online banking).

7 Make sure you choose a security outsourcer that you can trust fully, has proven competence and can guarantee consistent quality across locations.

8 In-house security departments often neglect to protect supply-side links into the network for cost reasons. Outsourcers will want to ensure effective protection at all levels, and may even be able to identify other cost savings in the process.

9 Effective IT security falls into three categories: confidentiality, integrity and availability (CIA). However, metrics should not be built around (unquantifiable) results, but around conformance to a standard like BS7799.

10 An ASP can provide effective protection against external threats, and offers considerable cost benefits for smaller organizations. However, larger organizations will need a functionally managed service which can also deal with internal threats.

11 Specialist IT security outsourcers currently offer the most comprehensive solution, but the larger generalist IT outsourcers are likely to catch up in future.

C H A P T E R 12

FACILITIES MANAGEMENT

For most businesses, outsourcing began with cleaning and catering, but facilities management (FM) followed close behind. It was a natural extension of the principle, combining buildings management, maintenance and some level of IT control. The attraction of FM as an outsourcing opportunity is simple – there are no ambiguities about core or non-core activities. Very few companies would list any of the typical FM contract components as anything other than peripheral to their business. A typical FM contract might include:

- ☐ Security.
- ☐ Cleaning.
- ☐ Maintenance of lighting, heating, air-conditioning and other electrics.
- ☐ Physical building maintenance (carpets, paintwork etc.).
- ☐ Fire management.
- ☐ Office redesigns (which, given that the average UK employee now moves desk every 18 months, is a significant headache for most companies).

Inevitably, the scope of these contracts is expanding as customers look for better value and suppliers look for new margin opportunities. In practice, however, evaluating this market is difficult because every provider from global multinational to local window cleaner seems to describe itself as a facilities management specialist. Many FM service providers that claim to deliver a holistic solution, in practice deliver their own core skills directly and manage sub-contractors to handle the remainder.

JOHNSON CONTROLS

One of the older companies in the Fortune 500, Johnson Controls has a remarkable ability for re-invention. It has an extraordinary financial track record, even through times of uncertainty. 2001 was the company's 55th consecutive year of sales growth and its 11th consecutive year of increased income. Its stock profile over the past ten years would shame even the most meteoric of IT superstars; take a look at the ten-year stock price chart in Figure 12.1.

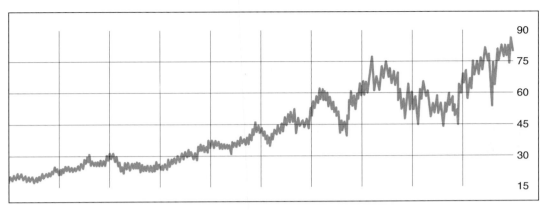

FIGURE 12.1: Johnson Controls's ten-year stock price chart

Through acquisition and streamlining, Johnson Controls now has two very different business streams, both underpinned by its engineering expertise (it started out as inventor of the central heating thermostat). One strand of the business is car seats and motor components, but it is the other which interests us – FM.

Johnson Controls positions FM as a high-technology service, centring around IT systems that integrate temperature control with computer-aided design, accounting solutions and performance measuring tools.

Like its competitors, Johnson Controls is always looking for new services to give it competitive differentiation. At the moment, it is leading the field of energy management services. Johnson claims a unique position, because it focuses on both supply-side and demand-side energy strategies. Supply-side services cover utility bill auditing, tariff auditing and negotiating with utilities to cut power costs. It sees a huge growth opportunity here as utility deregulation sweeps the globe. Demand-side energy management is based on the company's 50-year old practice of energy performance contracting. Johnson Controls audits environments to identify energy savings opportunities and builds implementation plans to deliver savings. Johnson's strategies range from the simple, like replacing current lighting systems, to the complex, such as using alternative fuel sources.

The company manages more than a billion square feet worldwide through its network of 300 locations worldwide.

SUMMARY

1 One of the first forms of outsourcing, FM is a combination of buildings management, maintenance and IT control covering functions like lighting, cleaning, building maintenance and security.

2 It is simple to implement, focusing as it does on clearly non-core business functions.

3 Everyone claims to be an FM provider, and the range of services offered continues to expand as companies fight for differentiation; however, most use sub-contractors to deliver non-core services.

CHAPTER 13

BUSINESS PROCESS OUTSOURCING

The usual customers for business process outsourcing (BPO) are large organizations looking to sharpen business focus on their core activities. With BPO, complete business divisions are managed by third parties – delivering products, services or dealing with customers. The outsourcer's core capabilities are built around these narrow business slices.

Unlike functionally managed service providers, BPO providers deliver their services with a complete infrastructure. That makes BPO projects politically complex and sensitive; for example, a service provider expecting to make its margin by improving IT systems risks comes into direct conflict with an internal IT group or incumbent IT outsourcer.

As with functionally managed services, an outsourcer will tailor its service for a particular client, using its specific processes and expertise to drive cost savings. BPO deals therefore tend to be very large to justify the set-up costs. This, of course, makes them very attractive for the providers.

We have already looked in detail at one good example of BPO. The iPSL case study (Chapter 6) explored how three major UK banks have shifted their entire cheque-processing operation over to a third party (albeit one in which they hold a considerable equity stake).

Organizations considering BPO need to weigh up such factors as:

☐ The nature of their partnership with the outsourcer.

☐ Risk sharing.

☐ The provider's track record.

☐ Cultural fit.

Such considerations are a far cry from the price-driven decisions to outsource IT or other business functions. They involve a great deal of analysis and careful planning. However, from a client's perspective, the end results can be worth all the effort. BPO, properly implemented, presents organizations with an opportunity for radical improvement, not simply more of the same at a lower cost.

TYPES OF BPO

Business service providers

Traditionally, business service providers (BSPs) have geared their services around smaller organizations looking for economies of scale. Call centres, for example, can offer smaller businesses the coverage and professional image of a corporation without the need for large headcount increases, shift-work management or technology infrastructure. Another huge growth area for BSP is HR.

Many large BPO contracts are joint ventures (see Chapter 20 for a discussion of the pros and cons of this approach).The outsourcer joins forces with the client to ensure the latter gets exactly the service it wants. However, once a service is up and running, it is common for the parties involved to identify further revenue opportunities and, over time, broaden the service to a number of other clients. On the basis of the chart (Figure 8.3), this changes what they are doing from BPO to BSP.

HR services

According to a 1999 report by research and analysis group Gartner Group/Dataquest, the worldwide market for integrated HR business process management services delivery is forecast to exceed $12 billion by 2003, which represents an astounding 88 per cent compound growth over 1998 figures.

One of the biggest names in HR outsourcing is Exult. Just two years old, the company has an impressive board line-up and has scored notable wins with Bank of America, BP Amoco and others. Indeed, at $600 million the BP Amoco deal was the largest deal of its type ever signed, secured in December 1999 when Exult was still a brand new company. The far-reaching contract was to 'create and operate for BP Amoco a comprehensive global HR services organization'.

The key contact at BP Amoco is quoted in an Exult press release as saying:

> *Through Exult's web-enablement of service delivery and its implementation of standardized HR services, we are gaining a holistic, practical and truly global service delivery solution that I firmly believe will allow us to usher in a new era of HR excellence.*

Despite the PR-speak, it is clear that HR outsourcing can deliver real benefits in cost, service and flexibility. There is always a risk involved in handing over the part of the business that is, after all, the interface between your company and its employees, to a third party. If staff really are your most important asset, abdicating responsibility for them is a brave move indeed! In practice, however, HR outsourcing should be about moving the humdrum, transactional business that forms the majority of HR activity over to a more efficient, structured model. This way, you free up the company's core HR knowledge-workers to develop better processes for staff selection, development and retention.

Call centres – the first frontier in business function outsourcing

For many organizations, business function outsourcing began with call centres in the mid-1980s. The success of this market has been overwhelming. Indeed, it is estimated that one in ten UK employees now works in a call centre, and the Call Centre Database (www.callcentredatabase.com) currently lists an astonishing 1,865 call centres.

The major vendors in the UK include:

☐ Organizations such as BT and Thus, for whom call centres have grown out of the core business.

☐ Generic outsourcing specialists such as Capita and ICL.

☐ Call centre specialists such as Merchants, Sitel and Sykes International.

The driver for this success was undoubtedly the strong natural fit for business function outsourcing. Typically, call centres were set up in-house by major consumer-facing organizations as a reactive base from which to field customer enquiries. As such they were seen as a cost centre whose real job was to shield the company from the trivia of dealing with customers' day-to-day problems. This is a dangerous line of reasoning. On this basis, the sole objective of the call centre is to get rid of the caller as quickly as possible, with no focus on the quality of the customer experience or resolution of the issue.

However, as the market matured, call centre outsourcing experts began to promise not only big savings, but also the ability to improve the customer experience – and maybe even generate some additional revenue.

OUTSOURCING SALES

Most management advice suggests that you should think very carefully before outsourcing elements of the business that affect the customer experience, since these are core activities. But a core activity is not necessarily a core competence. It is something that is central to your business, directly affects the customer experience and has the potential to add unique value. A core competence, meanwhile, is all of the above but must also be something that *you do best*. It may well be that a core activity can be handled better by a third party. If an outsourcer can provide a better quality of customer service than you, or drive higher sales, then you either need to improve your in-house function or consider outsourcing.

It is important to remember, however, that limitations in your capability may be due to the stage your business is at. For example, if your company was set up by operational staff and has grown by initial contacts, recommendations and reputation, you may not yet have built a strong sales force. But in a few years, you may want to take control and invest more heavily in the sales process. In other words, you need to think very carefully before you hand over the keys to your customer relationships.

On the other hand, how radical is sales outsourcing? Very few manufacturers of consumer durables, even those of very high value, handle customer relationships directly. They use networks of dealers, who can provide coverage without the manufacturer needing a vast portfolio of property or a huge, widely dispersed staff. The two most expensive purchases most of us ever make are our car and our house (indeed, research suggests that with global interest rates so low and consumer borrowing at a record high, the average UK household now spends more each month on their car than on their home loan. This trend is driven by both cultural and economic factors. Cars are more expensive in the UK than in most other countries, especially the US, and many European countries tend to see cars rather more rationally, as primarily a means of transport rather than emotionally, as a status symbol. That said, there is plenty of evidence to suggest a global shift towards the US/UK attitude towards the car as the most conspicuous demonstration of success). A brand-loyal car buyer is worth up to $750,000 to a manufacturer over a lifetime, yet we buy our houses from agents and most of our cars from franchised dealerships.

Sales outsourcing is therefore simply a logical extension of channel-based selling.

SUMMARY

1 Business process outsourcing (BPO) involves handing over the running of entire business divisions to third parties. Providers deliver bespoke services with a complete infrastructure. Contracts and customers tend to be huge.

2 Those considering BPO need to look beyond cost savings to other issues such as partnership and cultural fit. It requires detailed analysis and planning – but the results could be worth the effort.

3 Business service providers (BSPs) usually gear services around smaller organizations looking for economies of scale (e.g. call centres, HR services). BPO ventures often turn into BSPs as they capitalize on their infrastructure by offering their services to other organizations.

4 Outsourcing HR services should not negatively affect the interface between employer and workforce. By moving humdrum administrative HR activity out of the way, in-house HR staff are free to develop better processes for staff selection, development and retention.

5 Call centres were originally seen as cost centres, but the market has matured and service providers now promote the idea of call centres not only as a means to save money, but also to improve the customer experience and generate revenue.

6 A core activity is not the same as a core competence. The latter is something you do best, whereas a core activity may well be delivered more effectively by a third party.

7 Outsourcing sales activity is often seen negatively as handing over the customer relationship. While it certainly needs careful consideration, it is more sensibly viewed as a natural extension to traditional channel-based selling.

CHAPTER 14

INSOURCING

Insourcing is one of those words that management consultants were bound to invent sooner or later. Like most buzzwords, it means different things to different people, but is probably best defined as consolidating multiple, distributed operations into a single, geographically centralized group. This delivers similar functionality to the business as before, but as a separately managed entity, measured against service level agreements and accountable in a way similar to an outsourcer.

Insourcing has a number of advantages:

☐ It allows the business to maintain strategic control.

☐ It is relatively straightforward to go back if it does not work out.

☐ The business does not pay any margin to a third party.

☐ It provides a good opportunity to start the operation running at its optimum level, prior to outsourcing.

However, it also has some major disadvantages:

☐ Somebody has to be responsible for it, and the internal politics can become very complex.

☐ The financial constraints of your business are different to those of an outsourcer, so the new operation may not have the freedom to invest and operate as effectively as a third party.

☐ Insourcing arrangements may lack the formality of process that is a key driver for success in outsourcing relationships (the rest of the business is not seen as a 'real' customer).

☐ Geographical upheaval can cause a dramatic skills drain as relatively few staff are willing to relocate, especially if it is to another country and/or they are secondary wage-earners.

☐ The benefits of joining an outsourcing team for the staff are absent – they will see all the staff reduction, upheaval and inconvenience, but without any of the benefits.

Despite these cons, in some circumstances insourcing is the most appropriate way forward.

EXAMPLES OF INSOURCING

Unisys systems and technology division

In 1998, Unisys elected to insource the order-processing operations for its technology business. It coalesced the services around two shared service centres (SSCs), one on the west coast of the US and the other in Amsterdam. Previously orders were entered, managed and tracked at a country level. At the time, the company had also made a series of moves to get out of low-margin, commodity businesses (primarily PCs and the reselling of third-party equipment). Order volumes were falling dramatically, while the value of orders was climbing. The new approach enabled the company to streamline the process and save money.

Why not outsource? At the time, the company was running an extremely complex and outdated IT system (as is very often the case in IT companies). Some of the systems in use were written before the people who operated them were even born! Handling the integration challenges of connecting in a third party would have been phenomenally expensive. A rewrite would have been a lot more practical, but the company was already embarking on a complete corporate systems overhaul, replacing hundreds of interconnected systems with an integrated financial solution based on an off-the-shelf Oracle solution. Rewriting the systems for outsourcing would have only had a very short period for cost recovery before being replaced by the new Oracle services and, of course, a whole new set of connectivity challenges.

The SSC approach enabled Unisys to make significant savings and to build a model that was readily benchmarked and far more accountable to the business. In 2001, the company closed the Amsterdam centre and folded all the functionality into the US facility, driving further efficiencies.

ComputaCenter – an extraordinary business model

One of the success stories of the UK IT industry, ComputaCenter was founded in the early 1980s by a pair of Harvard Business School graduates, Philip Hulme and Peter Ogden. Despite its American spelling, the company is British through and through.

At the time, the PC industry was served almost entirely by computer dealers. The market was characterized by a huge population of small resellers and a handful of national chains (Entre, Interface, ComputerLand), the majority of which were franchised. ComputaCenter elected to run the whole business directly – something that served it well when margins in the PC industry began to suffer a severe and irreversible squeeze in the early 1990s.

Although the business is ostensibly run on a traditional distribution and resale model with directly employed salespeople, the nature of the relationship that ComputaCenter has with its sales force is unique.

Sales staff are given a very low basic salary – around a half to a third of the industry average – plus a reasonably generous stock option scheme. The commission they are paid is a straight percentage of the margin they make on their sales. The more they make for the company, the more they make for themselves. A small amount of tweaking of the bonus scheme keeps them focused on target products and services, but the principle is extremely simple.

So far, this does not sound like a particularly unusual commission scheme. What is unique, though, is that when a customer receives a non-paid-for service (such as technical support beyond the contracted service level, or presales resources), the salesperson is cross-charged, with the cost being taken directly from his or her salary. The salesperson can then decide whether to bill the customer, or to swallow the cost personally. If a salesperson believes that bringing in the chief executive of ComputaCenter is going to help clinch an important deal, he or she has the option to do so – but is billed personally for a day of the CEO's time!

Salespeople who have a large account to manage or a wide portfolio of smaller accounts may decide they need some kind of support to help. Any sales executive can hire an administrator, internal sales executive, assistant or secretary if they wish. The company will pay a small percentage of the salary of the new employee, the salesperson pays the rest. This means that staff growth is driven by real business need, not by ambition, empire building or any other undesirable motive.

If this sounds onerous, it is; an unsuccessful salesperson can leave ComputaCenter not only without any commission, but actually owing them money. The upside, however, is that successful ComputaCenter salespeople are extremely generously rewarded. They also enjoy an enormous amount of autonomy – the commission scheme ensures that they will operate broadly within the company's interest, and they are free to operate very much like a franchisee.

ComputaCenter has built by far the most successful computer reseller business in the UK, and now dominates the market. Its most successful sales staff have proved remarkably loyal, and the company has a high proportion of long-term employees who thrive on the culture and enjoy their autonomy (and their incomes).

Has the company outsourced sales? No, because it still employs the staff and has a sales management infrastructure. But the sales force is largely autonomous. Effectively, ComputaCenter has found a way to build a network of internal sales agents: an insourced third-party sales network.

SUMMARY

1 Insourcing means centralizing multiple, distributed business operations into a semi-autonomous unit. This is managed separately and accountable to the business like an outsourcer would be, but remains under the organization's control.

2 The pros of insourcing are: the business maintains strategic control; it is reversible; you avoid third-party margin costs; it can pave the way for full outsourcing.

3 The cons are: it is politically complex; you may not be able to match the financial efficiencies of an external provider; a lack of formal processes can impede success; staff may be unwilling or unable to relocate; staff suffer the downsides of upheaval without gaining any of the benefits of joining a large outsourcer.

4 However, it can be an appropriate strategy. Unisys's insourcing of the order-processing operations for its technology business enabled the company to streamline operations; ComputaCenter's franchise-like, insourced sales model has helped make it the UK's most successful computer reseller.

CHAPTER 15

APPLICATION
SERVICE
PROVIDERS

The concept behind application service providers (ASPs) is simple. They will run your IT applications on their systems, on your behalf. All your users will connect to the ASP's systems, usually via the internet. The ASP therefore delivers a service similar to IT outsourcing, but on a completely standardized basis, therefore cutting cost and shortening implementation time. Contracts are relatively simple to negotiate, availability is handled at the data-centre – the applications are all run from there. In the event that a failure is caused by a local machine breaking, the local device simply has to be swapped out for a new one. There is no reconfiguration to be done and no installation work – just plug in and go.

ASPs promise all the benefits of outsourcing, with none of the complexity. Yet despite having generated considerable hype, ASPs had a rough ride in 2002, with poor take-up and notable business failures. So why haven't they taken off?

The first problem lies with the gap between promise and delivery. In practice, delivering a wide portfolio of applications to many users from a single data-centre is extremely complex. The majority of high-profile ASPs attempted to launch onto the market with an offer built around just one or two applications. For example, a number would offer to deliver your e-mail service on a 'cost-per-user-per-month' basis. The problem with this is that the client is still left with the rest of its applications to manage and deliver. As a result, it has to pay once for its entire internal infrastructure and again for ASP services for the odd application. The ASP services may be cheaper, but if they are in addition to existing costs, there is no advantage. In short, it doesn't stack up.

Many ASPs talked of widening their portfolio as their customer base grew, but the growth never came. As the market started to question the value of high-tech stocks (especially internet stocks), the ASPs ran out of road.

The second problem they faced was their sales channel. Most attempted to sell their services through existing computer resellers. In practice, this was problematic. A typical reseller's business is built as much on turnover as on profitability. The business plan for most was to start niche, grow big and sell out. Anything that undermined the flow of revenue through the books was unattractive. Given the choice between a £100,000 order today and a revenue stream of £5,000 a month, practically no reseller would opt for the latter.

As we saw in Chapter 11, ASPs delivering services via the internet also face the accusation that they cannot offer true service guarantees – even with leased-line connections and quality-of-service (QoS) provisions in place, they do not have ultimate control over the performance of the backbone. This will change as standard internet protocols evolve to include better QoS provisions; but for many ASP businesses, it is already too late for that.

With a reluctant sales channel and a product that did not meet the needs of the customer, it is no surprise the model failed. But is the ASP concept doomed? The principle is still sound – outsourcing application provision offers benefits of simplicity and economies of scale. The challenge to ASPs is to deliver a complete solution, not just a partial suite of applications.

The alternative approach is a more complex business mix. UK outsourcing specialist ITNet has a strong focus on local government. ASP is just one part of a total service it offers its clients; other parts of that service are delivered along more traditional lines. ITNet's approach grew out of a single contract to provide a total IT outsourcing service to the London Borough of Enfield (see case study, Chapter 39). Enfield needed to implement an SAP solution to meet targets for e-government. ITNet decided to build the system in its own data-centre and connect the Enfield users remotely using thin-client technology. This meant that Enfield obtained the application without having to build extra capacity into its own facilities. The location of the servers was irrelevant to the council as the entire IT delivery service would be ITNet's problem.

ITNet now had a replicable service it could sell to other clients. Enfield became not just a valued customer, but a hub of strategic direction. The client became more important to the outsourcer (with all the associated benefits of management focus), and the outsourcer developed a new revenue stream.

Subsequently, ITNet has successfully sold its SAP ASP service to a number of other clients, and has widened the portfolio to cover other enterprise software applications. The ASP option allows it to mix the delivery methods to gain competitive advantage.

ONLINE CRM SERVICES

One field where ASP has bucked the trend of poor take-up is in sales force automation. Here it is seen as a natural fit. Most organizations have recognized that putting tighter processes around their sales operation results in significant improvements in both revenue and profits. For many, this drive for process improvement has become synonymous with the implementation of customer relationship management (CRM) software. The relative merits of this approach are outside the scope of this book, but it is clear that CRM implementation is fraught with difficulty.

According to a *ComputerWorld* article (December 2001)[1]:

> ❨ Despite lots of money (typically $5000 a seat and $2–5 million per deployment), many companies haven't seen a return on their CRM installations. Gartner estimates that 50 per cent of the installed CRM systems don't fulfil their promises. ❩

[1] Pimm Fox, 'CRM Nightmare Will Go Away', in *ComputerWorld*, 7 December 2001.

The article cites complex data translations, new hardware requirements, software licence costs and – the greatest challenge of all – behavioural change programs for the sales force itself.

One large software company elected to implement a global CRM solution under the exciting banner, Project Missouri. Within a couple of months it became universally known as Project Misery. In short, CRM sounds great, but implementation is very expensive, slow and politically divisive since staff are expected to change behaviour upfront with very little to show for their efforts until full implementation is complete – often months, or even years, later.

EXAMPLES OF ASPS

Salesforce.com

Salesforce.com claims world leadership in online CRM products. Started in Autumn 1999 by former Oracle executive Marc Benioff, the company delivers sales force automation and CRM technology as an ASP. Astonishingly, it claims to have around 4000 customers – not bad in such a short time.

Like his former Oracle colleague Tom Siebel, founder of Siebel Systems, Marc saw the explosive opportunity for CRM, but recognized complexity was a major stumbling block for implementation. (Interestingly, Larry Ellison, founder and CEO of Oracle Corporation, is himself listed as a major shareholder in Salesforce.com. Benioff was also a founding shareholder in Siebel Systems. Who says IT is an incestuous industry?)

Certainly web-based CRM holds out the promise of extraordinarily fast implementation. Salesforce.com's website quotes Joe DiDamo, a sales director at travel guide company Berlitz GlobalNet:

> Within a week of learning about Salesforce.com we were able to get five salespeople to check out the free trial, use the service to create customized sales reports, show the results to the CEO and decide to deploy the system worldwide.

It is hard to imagine a Siebel, Oracle, Onyx or Pivotal customer making a similar boast. Salesforce.com claims a typical ROI is more than 300 per cent in the first year.

Interviewed by Bloor Research's 'Jack of Diamonds' on IT-Analysis.com in April 2002, Beniof strikes a remarkable contrast to the rather chastened tones of most IT executives still grappling with the post-dotcom meltdown:

> We have grown substantially since our launch in 2001 when we hit the streets with the first online sales force automation and CRM products. Today we've got 4000 businesses out there using our software, including the likes of Siemens, Alcatel and USA Today. Le Meridien Hotels has more than 220 seats, Paymentech has more than 500.

We are the fastest-growing CRM company in the market, we're turning out great products and we are the only ASP out there making money. In 2001 we grew revenues by 300 per cent. The fourth quarter of 2001 saw us hit $7 million revenues and we are definitely not slowing down this year. By the end of 2005 I fully expect us to top revenues of $50 million. I believe that we have more active installations than all of the CRM firms combined.

Upshot

Another web-based CRM provider, the somewhat smaller Upshot, makes similar claims. Its focus is described as 'democratizing sales force automation'. It sees the opportunity to bring the technology out of the corporate market to a far broader base. This apparent small and medium enterprise (SME) focus is belied by its customer list. This includes some pretty substantial organizations, including Hewlett Packard's Enterprise Computing business group where Upshot claims to have successfully rolled out its service to 500 salespeople in just three weeks. In fact, Upshot guarantees to have its clients up and running within 15 days.

SUMMARY

1   ASPs run IT applications on their systems on your behalf, cutting costs and complexity.

2   The model has so far largely failed to take off. This is largely down to a reluctant sales channel and the ASPs' inability to deliver a broad enough portfolio of applications to meet customer needs.

3   Another area where ASPs are doing well is sales force automation and online CRM (e.g. salesforce.com, Upshot). Here they can dramatically simplify, speed up and cut the cost of delivering solutions that are notoriously complex, time-consuming and expensive to implement in-house.

CHAPTER 16

CONCLUSION

ANY COLOUR AS LONG AS IT IS GREY

By now you will have realized that categorizing outsourcing strategies is far from black and white. Guy Warren, VP of Service Delivery at Unisys, suggests two useful questions to ask:

- ☐ Does the CEO care about the metrics that come back from the process?
- ☐ Are the metrics based on business results?

If the answer to these questions is yes, then it is a business process; if not, it is a business function.

For example, is HR a business function or a business process? For most companies, HR is tightly bound into the full service delivered to clients. It is supported by other business functions such as finance and IT. After some agonizing, I decided to list it as a business process.

But, as we have seen, the economic viability of business process outsourcing deals are often predicated on the outsourcer being able to achieve long-term economies of scale. This suggests that the outsourcer plans to capitalize on investments it has already made to support additional clients. As soon as this happens, the relationship changes from one-to-one to one-to-many. At this point, arguably it is no longer a BPO contract, but business service provision or even ASP.

In practice, decisions regarding the business model often emerge naturally as the needs of both client and outsourcer become clear during discussions – but it is certainly sensible to have a thorough knowledge of all the options open to you.

Part 2 finishes with a case study that, among other things, effectively illustrates this decision-making process in action (see Chapter 17), before moving on to the challenges of practical outsourcing in Part 3.

CHAPTER 17

CASE STUDY: ABBEY LIFE AND UISL

Unisys Insurance Services Limited (UISL) is led by Peter Thomas, a former English teacher and financial services executive. Before being headhunted to run the company, Peter held a series of roles in marketing, customer services and business transformation at LloydsTSB, NatWest and Aon. As well as experience and credibility, Peter brought an extensive contact base. In this case study, we take a look at the goals he set staff and management and the way he has focused the business on very clear objectives.

ABBEY LIFE

Insurance company Abbey Life is no stranger to acquisitions. In 1988, the company was acquired by Lloyds Bank (as it then was). Ten years later, in 1998, Abbey Life itself moved into the acquisition game, snapping up Hill Samuel (which in turn had absorbed Target Life in 1995).

As the LloydsTSB empire expanded, the bank also took over Scottish Widows, and elected to make the company its single life and pensions brand, sitting alongside Cheltenham & Gloucester as the single mortgage service.

Abbey Life had a direct sales strategy that was, in the end, overtaken by competitors who sold through a network of independent financial advisors (IFAs). In 2000, Abbey Life closed the book on new life and pensions business.

At this time, the company was faced with two choices – either sell the closed-book business to a third party like Windsor Life (which was building a portfolio of closed-book pensions), or keep the business and run it at the lowest possible cost. After an initial study, it became clear a sale would only realize a proportion of the value, so instead the company set out to find an outsourcing partner to run the book on its behalf.

Abbey Life went to seven potential providers before settling on Unisys. At the time, Unisys was a surprising choice as it was a new market entrant. Despite extensive experiences in cheque processing (see iPSL case study, Chapter 6) and IT outsourcing, Unisys had no track record in the life and pensions business.

At the time of the tender process, Abbey Life faced three challenges:

☐ With a closed book, it had to find a way of maintaining staff morale while operating a business model that could only shrink the operation over time.

☐ Because of its acquisition history, the company was operating 18 separate legacy systems to service the different products in its portfolio.

☐ Euro-compliance deadlines were looming, and the company feared it would have to invest heavily in the development of systems that it had no wish to fund further.

Abbey Life invited tenderers to show how they would be able to generate guaranteed savings in excess of 20 per cent, and develop and implement an IT strategy that would simplify its legacy systems.

THE BUSINESS MODEL

Despite the apparent success of the iPSL joint venture, Abbey Life and Unisys elected not to go down the same route. Instead, Unisys set up a dedicated subsidiary to handle the service delivery – UISL.

Why not? Peter Thomas, managing director, says: 'None of the tendering companies proposed a joint venture to the point of a fully developed business case – it just wasn't the best fit for this requirement.' There were five principal reasons for this:

1 For Abbey Life, the most important issue was guaranteed pricing, and this could be more clearly measured if the supplying company was not connected to it financially.

2 The nature of the closed-book business meant that the company's priority was containment and risk transfer. A joint venture would have shifted some of the risk back to LloydsTSB, albeit indirectly.

3 The simplicity of a straight supplier deal was attractive.

4 Ultimately, for Unisys there was a significant revenue opportunity to offer a similar service to the rest of the market. There are 75 million closed-book policies in the UK and, as Thomas admits: 'Frankly, we would rather not share the revenue as we start to capitalize on that huge opportunity.'

5 In practice, 85 per cent of joint ventures between outsourcers and clients never win another client. This is usually because of concerns about competitive trust, or irreconcilable conflicts of interest between the founding partners and new venture. The UISL business model was heavily dependent on the company winning new business, so making it a joint venture would have introduced unnecessary risk.

Unisys already supplied one of the market-leading insurance software systems (Unisure), as well as a significant proportion of the large hardware systems on which such packages ran. In line with all other large hardware and software companies, Unisys's strategy was to turn itself into predominantly a services company to meet the needs of a changing economy. It made perfect sense for the company to develop its services for a sector in which it already had considerable experience – insurance.

Governance

UISL is very heavily ordered by service level agreements. There were initially more than 80 separate metrics, which were tracked every month. This was matched with an extremely precise and detailed statement of work that defined the responsibilities of both Abbey Life and UISL.

Sitting above the documentation is a tiered governance structure. At an executive level, there is a regular review by an executive steering group, which includes Peter Thomas and Ian Thompson, managing director of Abbey Life. Underneath this sit a number of specialist teams which meet regularly, including an IT forum and a compliance and audit forum. In each case, staff are matched one-to-one from each side of the partnership.

Peter Thomas says:

> ‘The governance structure is almost certainly over-engineered, but I like to see that in the early stages of an agreement. The client has to have confidence in the supplier, and until the track record is established, the governance structure is all it has. Six months into the contract we started an ongoing process of simplification. As with most outsourcing contracts, the service levels we have to meet are considerably higher than were being attained before. Once Abbey Life had confidence we could meet the new standard, things started to relax. ’

Simplification is important for both parties. As well as the obvious administrative overhead associated with complex measurement and reporting, it is important to allow the client to shift from managing the activity to managing the outsourcer.

THE FIRST YEAR – 2001

Peter Thomas's first priority was to turn the new venture into a ‘market-facing entity’ which could sell the same services to a wider customer base. He explains:

‘We wanted to turn UISL from a contract into a business with annuity revenues and a growing capital asset. Apart from the obvious commercial advantages to Unisys, we recognized that this was the way in which we would dramatically improve the working environment for staff. Administering a shrinking business is pretty soul-destroying.

By setting out to grow the business, staff can share in the satisfaction of being a core part of a growth engine, not just a non-strategic overhead. It is important to recognize that, in a shrinking business, people will inevitably leave when they can – and may prove difficult to replace. Alone, Abbey Life faced the risk of skills degradation that UISL's business growth plans could reverse. Now we have to choose whether, as we take on new business, we feed in through the Abbey Life offices in Bournemouth or add a second facility. ’

Peter set himself and his management team four objectives for year one:

1 Establish the service.

2 Completely re-focus the staff.

3 Establish a new cost base.

4 Commence the transformation work-stream.

The transformation work-stream is the IT and organizational overhaul that will drive the biggest cost savings. Peter intends to migrate 85 per cent of the policies from the 18 legacy systems to a single, Unisure-based system. The remaining 15 per cent are deemed too complex and arcane to be worthwhile migrating – it is cheaper to handle them as exceptions. The problem with this is that for the first two years, the costs vastly outweigh the benefits. Peter forecasts that the transformation will only cover its costs in the third or fourth year of the contract. This early investment requirement put significant pressure on UISL to make big savings elsewhere.

Peter's first task was to rearrange the Abbey Life facility in Bournemouth so that all the UISL staff were in a single building. Although only 1000 staff transferred over to UISL under TUPE (see Chapter 26), this task involved over 2000 separate desktop moves.

He then set a management challenge to increase productivity by 25 per cent in the first year. Peter believes that building new relationships with managers calls for setting short-term goals. 'Even for very senior guys with several hundred staff reporting in to them, I start out with monthly goal-setting. Over time, the scope expands as we come to understand one another better,' he says.

For the staff, he had a very clear message: 'To win new business, we need a delighted Abbey Life and a track record of delivery.' Everyone understood that winning new business was a key target, and this gave staff a fresh focus.

Given that there was no business growth, a 25 per cent productivity improvement could only come about by a 20 per cent staff cut. The management team elected to close a satellite facility in Croydon. This ran the Target Life and Hill Samuel life books, and was using different systems and processes to the Bournemouth operation. Staff at Croydon always knew closure was on the cards – the site had been under threat for around five years. This made the transition easier than might be expected. All staff were offered relocation to Bournemouth (although, not surprisingly, only one accepted).

Peter Thomas says: 'Unisys also recognized the value in being able to show the market we could shift two very different life books into the Abbey Life facility in Bournemouth – our first reference case.' Peter set a target of 12 months to handle the transition, within a budget and without any drop in service level. 'While we did not necessarily handle the transfer in the same way as we might with others, the process was very efficient,' he says.

The company started out by building a new team to handle the policies out of Bournemouth. It recruited two-thirds of the team from outside, focusing on people aged 18 to 21. The rest of the team was made up of experienced staff who could coach others and lead the operation.

Training was handled at three levels: formal training courses, one-to-one coaching and shadowing staff at the Croydon office for six to ten weeks.

How were the Croydon staff kept motivated enough to execute the handover? Peter Thomas explains:

❝ We started with a briefing for all the staff in groups. I ran every briefing session personally and offered a one-to-one briefing, again personally, to every single member of staff. They were kept fully informed at all times – the news may not have been good, but it was open, honest and up-to-date. Each staff member was then offered a retention bonus to stay through the handover period. Abbey Life was not unionized, but the bonuses were agreed through formal staff representation. We also agreed a suite of outplacement services.

Next, I set them a professional challenge. I told them: "There is a right way and a wrong way to do this. I'd like to see you hand over the work in near perfect order." The psychology of this approach was to ensure that, although they knew they were leaving, they would also know their work was important, measurable and valued by the company. It gave them something to aspire to through this difficult time.

Meanwhile, the new staff had to spend a lot of time away from home, so we put them up in a very nice hotel with excellent leisure facilities to show them how important they were to us. We set individual training plans and made them all readily visible. At the end of the process we ran success dinners in both Croydon and Bournemouth for all concerned. At a management level, we ensured that the old and new management teams had the same objectives – skills transfer, service levels and customer satisfaction. *

Did it work? 'Well, the transfer was completed four months early, within budget and well within service-level demands.'

THE SECOND YEAR – 2002

Year two is often the hardest – the buzz and excitement of the initial launch has faded, there are still organizational issues to sort out, and it can all seem a bit business-as-usual. For UISL, Peter Thomas again set clear objectives:

- ☐ Sustain and improve service levels.
- ☐ Continue the transformation work-stream.
- ☐ Transfer staff to the new company's improved performance measurement system (where it makes sense).
- ☐ Win new business.

Winning new business was never on the cards for the first year of trading – there was no track record of delivery and the sales cycles are at least six to nine months, so there was little time. In year two, however, the business must prove its sustainability. The goal is to win one major account. UISL believes it can handle up to three, since it has a ready pool of resources back at Unisys. Finding operational staff is never a problem with outsourcing deals because they transfer along with the rest of the resources; typically the difficulty is finding agents of change and experts in systems integration. Unisys's core business means that there is a ready supply of these skills, hence its ability to work for multiple clients simultaneously.

UISL – THE FUTURE

The top priority for UISL is to win more closed-book pensions business. With a market of 75 million policies, it sees tremendous growth potential. Beyond that, it can look at open-book pension administration and ultimately a wider brief of broad-based, white-collar outsourcing. Management guru Tom Peters suggests that over 90 per cent of white-collar workers are at risk of outsourcing,[1] so the level of opportunity is clear.

[1] Tom Peters, *Professional Services Firm 50*, Alfred A Knopf, 1999.

3

PRACTICAL OUTSOURCING: HEAD DOWN, HANDS ON

CHAPTER 18

GETTING
STARTED

It is the first warm day of spring 2002 and I am sitting in a café with an old friend who has just become Operations Director for a large division of a top-20 retailer. Now the company car has been selected and the basic operational business is under control, what is the first real task? One of the units within his remit is critical to the business but unprofitable. It looks inefficient and needs a radical overhaul. Should it be outsourced and, if so, how and to whom?

Notebook in hand, I ask him about the issues he is facing. The stream of questions comes back without him even pausing for breath – an indication of both the size of the challenge and the power of caffeine:

‹Do I choose a single supplier and keep it simple or split my risk and go multi-vendor? Should I run a full tender process and, if so, how do I resource it, how do I find out how to do it and where do I get the right people? I am already overrun with consultants – who do I need and how do I choose? What do I do about metrics, reviews and service level agreements? How do I decide between expensive, arrogant blue-chips and more aggressive, likeable, but smaller specialists? If I prefer the smaller player, how do I sell the decision to the board? How many suppliers should I go and see – and how short should the shortlist be? How do I project-manage the changeover? How do I assess the risks and the costs? I am beginning to realize that the devil really is in the details, but which details? What exactly are we buying? How do we assess and score the responses once we get them in? How do we know that the vendor we choose is really going to deliver? How do we find out whether it shares our values? How do we get enough transparency to understand what we are paying for? Is this whole project strategic or tactical – and do I really have a vision for it? How long am I making this commitment for?›

My friend's confusion is shared by many people who find themselves in the position of having to kick off an outsourcing evaluation. This part of the book will show you how to find the right answers to these questions. A good guiding principle is neatly summed in the famous quotation from Stephen Covey:

‹The main thing is to keep the main thing the main thing.›[1]

[1] Stephen Covey, *The 7 Habits of Highly Effective People*, Simon & Schuster; 1989.

Once you have decided on an outsourcing route, you then have to ask how you move from strategy to execution without diluting the original objectives. And, given the risks associated with outsourcing, how do you protect your interests? We will tackle these questions head-on, examining different approaches to negotiation, service level agreements and structures of governance that will enable your organization to get the best return for the lowest risk.

CHAPTER 19

THE NEGOTIATION PROCESS

Outsourcing contracts can either be built on the basis of getting the better of the deal, or on the basis of win-win. If your outsourcer is financially strong, your objectives are fully understood and entirely quantifiable, and you can be certain that the scope of the deal will not grow or change, it is theoretically possible to implement a classic procurement arrangement where your organization gets the maximum from the provider at the minimum cost.

In these situations, it is important to recognize that the outsourcer will invest considerable effort in finding ways of increasing margins. This will impact on:

☐ Flexibility.

☐ The way in which your former staff are treated.

☐ Customer service (potentially).

Ultimately, the outsourcer may be forced into a position where it tries to break the agreement – a move that could have an impact on reputation, management time and legal costs. In practice, this sort of win-lose deal fits only where the service being outsourced is highly commoditized. PC maintenance or office cleaning contracts are generally very easy to transfer from one supplier to another. Here there is little opportunity for differentiation between providers, so there is scope for aggressive contracting.

However, in the main (and certainly in the case of strategic outsourcing) win-win is almost always the most viable approach.

As with any other commercial negotiation, to put yourself in the best position you need to understand *all* of the supplier's opportunities to win. While the financial aspect will always be critical, there may be a strong driver around breaking into a new market, developing a reference site, developing repeatable solutions or consolidating its position as a leading supplier in a given market segment.

As a prospective client, you must establish early on what these opportunities are, and use that knowledge as a part of your engagement strategy. The more you know about the outsourcer's objectives, the better deal you are likely to strike for both parties. The same is also true in reverse. The outsourcer should be working hard to understand all of your objectives and areas of potential opportunity from the relationship. If it is not doing this, is it really the right partner for you?

Barlow Lyde & Gilbert (BLG) is an international law firm with offices in London, Oxford, Hong Kong and Shanghai. It specializes in outsourcing contract law, and counts both major outsourcers and many outsourcing clients among its customers. In the past 18 months, it has handled around $2.2 billion's worth of outsourcing agreements in transaction value.

David Strang, a partner in the outsourcing team, highlights the importance of due diligence, but points out how it differs from that required in most other business transactions. When preparing a business division for sale, for instance, there is a degree of responsibility on the part of the selling party to quantify what it owns and what is included in the sale, but ultimately it is the buyer who has to be certain of the details of the deal – *caveat emptor*. In an outsourcing arrangement, however, unpleasant surprises for the outsourcer will inevitably come back to bite the client. Successful outsourcing arrangements will be profitable for both parties. Those that favour either party over the other are unlikely to run their full course.

GETTING THE BEST FROM THE DEAL

Negotiating an outsourcing contract involves a significant investment of time, from beginning to end. Even at the selection stage, it is worthwhile entering the process with the aim of helping each prospective supplier to put forward the best, most relevant offer possible. Outsourcing advisor Orbys makes it clear that a client has to do almost as much of a selling job as the potential service provider. Bob Aylott, a principal consultant at Orbys, says:

> ❛ Don't enter into negotiations on the basis that you are shopping around for a service. It is important to sell yourself and your own organization to the outsourcing provider. ❜

The more opportunity the prospective outsourcer can see for kudos or future revenue growth, the better the deal it will want to put together. The more it likes working with you, the harder it will work to secure the deal. And the more impressed it is with the potential of your operation, the better deal you are likely to get when it comes to negotiating risk/reward later in the process.

This is particularly true in the UK public sector, where competitive tendering rules and initiatives such as PPP and PFI can lead to very high pre-sales costs which will deter many companies from bidding. Here the key is to attract the right bidders and keep them in the process to ensure you have the best possible choice. There is a real danger that a preferred supplier may drop out at any point in the selection process – even at best and final offer pricing (BAFO) stage. For a wider view of public sector behaviour in other markets, see Part 4, Chapter 32.

Rob Watt, managing director of outsourcer ITNet's commercial division, recommends assessing how important you would be to the outsourcer as a client by asking yourself a series of questions:

☐ If you are going to be an outsourcer's biggest customer by far, does that mean it cannot be flexible over the contract without damaging its balance sheet?

☐ If you are going to be a small account, how often will you see the outsourcer's best people once the contract has been secured?

☐ Are you in a line of business which is strategic to the outsourcer? If so, can you benefit from the provider investing in new applications that it hopes to sell to others?

☐ Are you in a line of business which is outside the outsourcer's normal sphere of operation? If so, does it plan to develop a new line of business around you? If so, can you capitalize on this move by proposing a gain-share on future wins in return for acting as a reference? If not, do you really want to be in that position?

Phil Morris, a main board director at outsourcing expert Morgan Chambers, describes negotiation as: 'The process of getting your original objectives from a deal.' Morris advises clients to negotiate on the issues of service, quality, financial objectives and people. Only when the content of a deal has been agreed should you discuss price. Morris advises a very structured approach. Agreeing large-scale outsourcing contracts can take between six and nine months, so you really need to appoint a dedicated, specialist contract-negotiation team.

Outsourcing a problem

Commonly held management theory suggests that you should not outsource a problem, as you are only likely to make matters worse. Indeed, the old computing axiom 'garbage in, garbage out' applies: if you hope to shift a dysfunctional process over to a third party without careful planning, you are probably in for a torrid time.

However, outsourcing a problem is in fact a perfectly effective way to solve it, as long as that problem is recognized and understood by all parties. If the outsourcer is on the ball during negotiations, it may well identify unforeseen difficulties. If you fail to acknowledge these, then you will find the proposed costs prohibitive and the negotiation process unpleasant. Even worse, if the outsourcer only finds out about a problem once it has taken over, it will be forced to apply every measure it can to recoup costs or renegotiate service levels down.

However, if the problem is recognized, characterized and sized, outsourcing may be the best way to tackle it. This is particularly the case where a problem needs early capital investment, but lies in a non-revenue-creating part of the business.

Outsourcing consultants

Organizations like Orbys and Morgan Chambers have built substantial practices by helping organizations entering into outsourcing agreements get the best deal. Are they worthwhile?

Bob Aylott from Orbys argues that an experienced outsourcing negotiator ought to be able to save a client at least 5 per cent over the lifetime of a contract. If the deal is worth $15 million a year, over five years that 5 per cent represents a saving of $3.75 million. Given the average engagement costs under $1.5 million, this seems good value for money.

Morgan Chambers, the largest outsourcing consultancy, focuses on longer-term engagements, having extended its services to the SLA and contract review process. It argues that this approach gives it the flexibility to charge on the basis of results rather than just time and materials.

With all that lost revenue, you might think outsourcers would consider these consultants a bunch of parasites eating away at their margins. ITNet's Rob Watts says:

' Actually, no. Where an organization is entering into an outsourcing agreement for the first time, we like to see outsourcing consultants in place. An experienced negotiator can help the client keep problems in perspective and recognize the important issues. Inexperienced negotiators often focus on relatively unimportant areas and find key decisions difficult to make in a timely manner. They lack the experience to understand that many concerns can be resolved through good SLA development and a strong governance process.

We would not be as enthusiastic about outsourcing consultants where there is a high level of experience already in the client's team. In those situations, there is a risk that the consultant can do no more than slow things down by introducing spurious hurdles in order to demonstrate their "added value". '

Watts recommends that consultants are introduced where they can simplify, rather than complicate processes. Once basic selection is out of the way, the outsourcing consultant should bring the two parties together and ensure each understands the other's objectives. If they are standing in between, then they will probably be doing more harm than good.

Telling the staff

One of the greatest challenges is timing the best moment to tell the staff what is going on. Speak too early, when the deal is still uncertain, and you could expose them to a great deal of concern and heartache over a change that never occurs. Leave it too late and you will not have the negotiation flexibility to address genuine concerns. In addition, the longer you leave it, the more likelihood there is that you will face the worst-case scenario – that staff learn of the plans unofficially through the office grapevine.

Guy Warren, VP of service delivery at Unisys, advises that you should tell everyone as much as you can as early as possible, but be clear about what stage things are at.

As soon as the decision to outsource has been made public, the staff affected need to be told what is going to happen to them in as much detail as possible. To do this effectively, you will need the engagement and support of the prospective outsourcer. But bringing in a third party to brief staff early could put it in a stronger negotiating position than you would have liked – after all, once the provider has been introduced to the staff and set the expectation levels, it will be much harder for you to walk away from the deal. Warren proposes that you bring the outsourcer in anyway, but make sure that it is made clear to everyone what stage discussions are at. The outsourcer can be introduced as just one of many partners being considered, subject to due diligence, or as a preferred partner under active consideration. Everyone must be told clearly that the deal has not been finalized and may therefore not go ahead as described. For a more detailed discussion on this issue, see Chapter 31.

Ensuring compatibility

Many outsourcers make their code of ethics clear. Perot Systems, for example, issues all staff with a small card detailing the corporate values. This includes references to customer service, integrity, 'treasuring people' and 'rewarding stakeholders'. Such statements of values and ethics can be woolly and often tell you little about how the organization really operates.

However, the flip side of Perot's card outlines its corporate 'style'. And by understanding an outsourcer's style, you can start to take a view on how compatible its approach is with your own. For example, one section of Perot's card advises staff to 'encourage every team member to take risks, exercise initiative, deliver quality results, and never be afraid to make mistakes'. This approach is common to US corporations that want to encourage creativity, yet, as one ex-employee told me recently, it caused significant problems when it was picked up by a new client – a major European bank. The last thing the bank wanted to see was its service being delivered by people that were encouraged to make mistakes!

Articulating judgements

Some core requirements are impossible to measure, and these need to be assessed in another way. You need to articulate what you mean as unambiguously as possible, and it often takes an external agent to get the form of words absolutely right. (Companies like Orbys boast of their 'open process to help the client articulate its informed judgements'.) You can then go back to the supplier to qualify.

Whether you rely on a third party to guide you through the negotiation or elect to tackle the process yourself, it is important to lay out a strategy for evaluation of dissimilar bids and smooth handling of the transition from negotiation to integration.

Quantifying judgements

The next step is to quantify and qualify those judgements and turn them into tangible, defined objectives that can be made explicit in a contract.

For example, 'I want to improve my internal customer satisfaction levels' could become: 'Satisfaction surveys should be run on a regular basis, with expectations of improvements over time.'

Something like 'I want to see a reduction in fraud' needs more thought. There is always an argument that you do not know how much fraud is going on. But in banking, for example, if money is appearing in one place there is usually a shortfall somewhere else, and you can certainly apply metrics around shortfalls. Fraud reduction can be tackled by automation – reducing the number of people involved in any given transaction cuts the opportunity for misdemeanours. Further improvements can be made by improving screening in the recruitment process and by more effective management.

APPROACHING NEGOTIATION

It is important to recognize that if you are too aggressive over service levels with the outsourcer in negotiation, you will simply pay more. Where contracts are overly onerous, suppliers have to indemnify themselves against risk either by building in extra margin or offsetting the risk though financial engineering or indemnity insurance. Either way, costs increase and the whole contract becomes less transparent.

Over-aggressive negotiation does not just affect the cost, but also the complexity. It is usually far better to understand exactly how the costs are built up, rather than forcing the supplier to engage in heavy financial engineering that is difficult to unpick and prevents you from understanding precisely what you are paying for.

Once you can understand both your own objectives and exposure to risk and those of the supplier, you can make better-informed judgements and negotiate more effectively.

At the same time, it is critical that you do not underestimate the value of your own resources. David Strang of Barlow Lyde & Gilbert gives an example:

'If you have a substantial data-centre that is only running at 30 per cent capacity, an outsourcer may choose to apply that spare capacity elsewhere to satisfy demand for another client. Is that acceptable to you without you receiving any royalties or revenues? Is the outsourcer entitled to run software developed in-house (or on your behalf) for another client – possibly a competitor?'

All these matters are straightforward to resolve, but only if they are identified and addressed at the beginning of the relationship.

SUMMARY

1 Win-win is almost always the best approach to outsourcing deals.

2 To put yourself in the best negotiating position, understand *all* of the supplier's opportunities to win. Likewise, the outsourcer should understand all your objectives and areas of opportunity.

3 Sell the opportunities of your organization to the outsourcing provider, so that it will work harder to secure the deal. This is particularly true in the public sector, where bureaucratic processes and high pre-sales costs can deter companies from bidding.

4 Contrary to popular belief, you *can* outsource problems – as long as they are recognized and understood in advance by all parties.

5 Appoint a dedicated negotiation team. Using outsourcing consultants may be a good move if you are not experienced in outsourcing negotiations. However, for more seasoned outsourcing clients, they can get in the way.

6 Tell staff what is happening as soon as possible. It can be advisable to introduce them to potential outsourcers, but it should be made clear exactly what stage the deal is at – you do not want to prejudice negotiations.

7 Judge whether the outsourcer's organization is compatible with your own by understanding its company values and style.

8 Identify the 'must-haves', articulate your requirements clearly (possibly using a third party) and translate them into quantifiable objectives that can be made explicit in a contract.

9 Over-aggressive negotiation over service levels leads to increased cost and complexity, but do not underestimate your position either – there could be substantial revenue opportunities in which you can share.

CHAPTER 20

PARTNERSHIP AND PRICING MODELS

FIXED-PRICE OUTSOURCING

Fixed-price outsourcing has a number of advantages if a service can be represented in a sufficiently granular fashion. A recent *McKinsey Quarterly* article[1] identified the European airlines' preference for buying on-board catering services on the basis of a fixed price per meal. The airlines set a price, the caterers propose a set of menus and the airlines make their selections.

Fixed-price contracts are cheap to write, easy to measure and implement and are reasonably straightforward to transfer should you need to change provider. The challenge with them is that you are asking the outsourcer to carry all the risk. In order to do that, the provider needs to build in contingency costs and have total control over the factors driving its cost base. If you seek to control *how* it delivers the service, you limit its ability to commit to fixed prices. Equally, if the service relies on your own resources (especially where costs or availability may fluctuate), fixed cost will be impractical to deliver competitively.

Fixed-price policies also limit the outsourcer's ability to use its creativity and introduce new ideas. By defining the service too tightly, you limit the opportunities that the outsourcer can bring. For simple contracts like cleaning or catering this may not be an issue, but in more strategic outsourcing environments, you are likely to create an environment where innovation and a balanced view of quality versus cost are actively discouraged.

GAIN-SHARE

According to Bob Aylott at Orbis, gain-share should always be based on added value, i.e. improvements in service beyond the core. 'Core delivery should be an absolute, controlled by the SLA. The added-value areas provide the scope for truly shared reward as they can represent incremental revenue for both parties,' he says.

[1] Byron Auguste, Yvonne Hao, Marc Singer and Michael Wiegand, 'The Other Side of Outsourcing' in *McKinsey Quarterly*, 2002 Number 1.

Guy Warren at Unisys argues it may be advantageous for the client to go for a value-sharing approach on the core deliverables for suppliers that perform well ahead of expectations, but he agrees that in functionally managed outsourcing – where the supplier is contracted to deliver against a reasonably tight SLA – there is little scope for risk/reward models.

JOINT VENTURES

Joint ventures (JV) are popular as they provide the client with a sense of control over the new enterprise. A feeling of lack of control is commonly the greatest source of dissatisfaction in outsourcing relationships, so the JV option sounds attractive. It does, however, pose significant risks. Apart from the rather poor track record in JV survival rates, a JV can easily leave the client facing irreconcilable competition between the new venture and the core business.

For example, let us look at a bank that chooses to outsource its cash handling and deliver the service via a JV. Initially, the service is charged back to the bank on a basis that covers the JV's costs. The bank sees an improvement in service level and a small reduction in cost. So far, so good. But for the JV to thrive, it must sign up other banks. To do so, it will need to be competitive and, with many of the costs already underwritten by the initial contract, it is likely to bid the service to the original bank's competitors at a price lower than the partnered bank is paying. Now the bank finds itself selling its own skills to its direct competitors at a cost lower than it is paying itself! Similar conflicts can also affect the outsourcer if the new JV starts to move into areas of competition with its main business.

Nevertheless, the JV approach offers four possible advantages:

1   Control.

2   For the banking industry, the possibility of some VAT advantages (see Chapter 4).

3   Capital gain.

4   Income generation.

In reality, control is almost universally the real motivation. A JV gives the client operational and management control of the service. Indeed according to Peter Thomas, managing director of UISL (see case study, Chapter 17), 85 per cent of JV outsourcing arrangements never find a second customer.

Aylott is sceptical about many JV enterprises. He argues that if you are entering into one, you should be looking for growth, but should also plan to sell out within five years. This keeps you focused on generating capital gain and dealing with conflicts.

In a JV, if the incentives are in place to grow the business, it is important to understand that you are explicitly encouraging certain behaviours. Before embarking on this approach, you should consider whether these are the behaviours you want to see in a contract.

Making risk/reward work

The key is to ensure that the risk/reward is structured to encourage the right behaviours. Any additional payments should be for value that has been added beyond the core outsourcing service – in other words, truly added value.

Orbys advises that a client should not pay enough on the basic outsourcing deal to satisfy the needs of the service provider outright. Instead, the outsourcer should be given an incentive to add value, in order to achieve or exceed its targets. The added value can be as variable or wide-ranging as you wish. For example, a local education authority may have a mandate to improve education within its regions. It may not have direct control over the pupils, but it is not unreasonable to expect to measure it on examination pass rates or rates of improvement. Likewise with risk/reward, Aylott advises incentivizing the outsourcer in areas where it has a significant influence, but which it may not ultimately be able to control.

You can never build a successful risk/reward model on the basis of costs saved. After all, if the supplier has found a way to deliver a service to you at a lower cost, why would it tell you? Accounting practices are simply too flexible to be able to track the true cost of anything when it is being delivered through a division of a larger company. Internal charges, write-down policies and retrospective discounting from providers all make it very easy for an outsourcer to present a given project as being as profitable as it chooses.

Economies of scale

As discussed earlier, economies of scale represent the single largest source of cost reduction in an outsourcing contract. But how do you capitalize on that when yours is the first contract of its type to be set up by the outsourcer? It is important to establish whether there is scope for the outsourcer to offer the service to others after it has signed up with you. If there is, part of the risk/reward process might be to agree to be a reference site, in return for a share of the savings as new clients come on board.

SUMMARY

1 For simple functions such as catering and cleaning, fixed-price contracts are easy to implement, measure and transfer. However, they are highly limiting and inappropriate for more strategic outsourcing contracts.

2 Gain-share should mostly be based on value added beyond the core service.

3 Joint ventures have a poor track record, and both client and outsourcer face risks of competitive conflicts with the core business. However, JVs offer the client more control and the possibility of revenue generation.

4 To be successful, a JV needs to be a true partnership: both sides must carry risk, make new revenue and focus on added value.

5 Risk/reward needs to incentivize the outsourcer to add real value in order to achieve or exceed its targets. You can never build a successful risk/reward model on the basis of costs saved.

6 If there are opportunities for the outsourcer to make economies of scale in future, part of the risk/reward process might be to agree to be a reference site in return for a share of the savings as new clients come on board.

CHAPTER 21

PROTECTING YOUR INTERESTS

REFERENCES

Any outsourcing company bidding for business will provide a list of references. It is vital that these are followed up in appropriate detail. For example, reading a case study will tell you of a client's satisfaction at a particular point in time. A thorough reference process, though, will involve a visit to the reference site and a frank and wide-ranging discussion that addresses questions of policy as well as portfolio. Key questions might include:

☐ How do you rate the service provider's attitude?

☐ How well is its culture aligned to yours?

☐ Is it easy to deal with or adversarial?

☐ Does the provider involve a contracts manager at every stage of the engagement? If so, what is his or her role?

RAPACIOUS CONTRACT ENFORCEMENT

Some outsourcers look to make their margin out of 'scope creep', i.e. they will encourage the client to ask for extra services as the contract proceeds and will make a hefty margin providing these. Alternatively, they will implement a contract to the letter and rely on the fact that essential services have not been contracted for.

How do you deal with this? You need to understand how the outsourcer is planning to make money from the contract upfront. If you push the supplier too hard, you will leave it no alternative but to scrap for revenue wherever it can.

Your protection comes from building in the measures you value and incentivizing the right behaviour. By using a mix of SLAs and KPIs (such as satisfaction) you should aim to build a contract where the supplier cannot squeeze one area without impacting its revenue somewhere else.

Rob Watt of ITNet suggests that, while you can never legislate for every likely requirement, it makes good sense to push for a schedule of costs for as many different service options as possible, and include this in the contract. This will at least enable you to limit the impact of hidden extra charges, and may also throw up areas you should be including in negotiation that may not have been apparent before.

ABUSE OF PENALTIES

You need to be very careful with the design of penalties in the SLA. For example, setting a three-day maximum delivery time for a new PC sounds reasonable. However, with no further metrics in place, once the outsourcer has missed the three-day deadline, it is better off holding back delivery until all the other machines in the queue are commissioned and delivered. That way it just pays a single penalty and does not waste any more time on the already-late order. This is fine for the outsourcer, but can lead to weeks of delay for the user – certainly not what the SLA was designed to deliver.

A similar problem can arise with availability guarantees where a figure is given for downtime per month. In a month where performance has been strong, the outsourcer may choose to implement forced downtime on the last working day of the month, in order to save itself out-of-hours work the following month.

Throughout the process of contract development, the key question is: how will this item affect the outsourcer's behaviour?

CONTRACT TERMINATION

As we have already seen, it is very difficult to consider bringing a function back into the organization once it has been outsourced. However, transition to another supplier is a little easier. The provisions of TUPE (see Chapter 26) ensure there is an obligation on the outsourcer to transfer the staff allocated to a given service over to a new employee when the contract changes hands. This is not, however, as simple as it may at first seem. An organization is unlikely to change outsourcing providers without a good deal of notice; the relationship will have turned sour or some kind of competitive tender process will have been undertaken, giving the incumbent plenty of warning of change.

There is very little to stop the outsourcer making personnel changes on that team at any point up to the termination of the contract. At its simplest, the outsourcer may choose to move a few of the best people onto different projects shortly before contract termination so that the bulk of people move over, but the best are kept back. A more malign outsourcer may choose to give substantial salary increases to all staff a week before contract termination. The TUPE rules state that employees transferring over to a new contract will keep all their existing terms and conditions of employment. If the contract is likely to go to a competitor, there is every incentive for the outsourcer to ensure that the competition loses money on the deal.

Such actions have to be legislated for contractually. David Strang, a partner in the outsourcing team at law firm BLG, advises the inclusion of a 'no monkeys' clause – a clause that states the outsourcer cannot change the staff or their terms and conditions without approval, or following notification of intent to consider a change of supplier.

Ultimately, despite all the talk of partnership and working together, it is vital that you plan sufficiently for contract termination (see Chapter 28).

UNIONS

Some outsourcing suppliers only work with unions if absolutely necessary. Others, such as Unisys, have a track record of embracing unions and working with them during transition processes and beyond. ITNet recognizes unions but does not enter into collective bargaining with them.

There are no rights or wrongs in any of this, but it is important to recognize that many clients choose to outsource precisely because of outdated or restrictive working practices, and they see the ability to move away from union-negotiated relationships as positive. Others may see the willingness of the third party to engage with unions as a valuable contribution to industrial relations across the rest of their business.

It is worth pointing out, however, that (especially in the UK public sector), the union will have significant impact whether or not it is recognized. Many public sector staff are paid salaries based upon nationally-negotiated pay awards. These agreements will form a part of their terms and conditions and are therefore enshrined in the TUPE agreement (see Chapter 26). Whether the union is directly engaged or not, salaries will be driven by union-negotiated pay deals.

Does the outsourcer's stance on unions matter? Only if you decide that an outsourcer's willingness to engage with the unions is important to you.

LIQUIDATED DAMAGES

'Liquidated damages' is the legal term for a form of tariff mechanism. At its simplest, it means 'if you do this, you pay that'. The idea is to take the assessment of damages out of the courts and replace them with a simpler matrix of fixed costs for non-performance.

The most common form of liquidated damages in an outsourcing contract is the service credit – a penalty for failure to perform against a pre-agreed SLA.

When constructing SLAs, there is an expectation that the outsourcer will incur some form of financial penalty if it fails to meet the performance levels agreed. But according to Simon Shooter, another partner at BLG, under English law you cannot enforce a fine or penalty against a third party. As such, incentives to perform must be carefully constructed. With a service credit, the client sees a reduction in its next invoice by the previously negotiated value should the service fail to meet expectations. If, however, the outsourcer believes it is being unfairly penalized (as per the contract or otherwise), it can take the matter to the courts, which will decide if the financial penalty represents a proper pre-estimate of the suffering incurred.

Shooter cites one of his former clients' advice for setting service credits: make the supplier squeak.

    ‘If the supplier has moved from squeaking to screaming, your penalties may not stand up in court. If you understand the suppliers' margins, you will have a good idea of where to set the service credits. Ideally, a service credit will take away the provider's margins, but will not force them into a loss-making position. In a typical IT outsourcing situation, margins run between 10–14 per cent, so setting service credits at 50 per cent is clearly unreasonable. ⟩

Not surprisingly, most suppliers dislike service credits, but are usually forced to accept them as a condition of getting a contract. Shooter feels that, in fact, service credits can operate in the outsourcer's long-term interest. By having a predetermined formula to deal with one-off problems, they can be isolated and resolved. He describes service credits as:

☐ Simple and bloodless.

☐ An alternative to initiating a full-scale dispute.

☐ A means of ensuring problems do not fester – the client is compensated and the outsourcer suffers, so the matter can be closed.

☐ A means of minimizing threats to the long-term relationship.

It is clearly the outsourcer's responsibility to ensure it can achieve the service levels to which it commits, and that it writes in some protection against failure to deliver due to outside forces. For example, the quality of service may be based on the delivery of a new application that is the responsibility of the client or is agreed under a separate contract. In this case, the service can be agreed to apply at one level before the system goes live and another, higher level afterwards.

CONSEQUENTIAL LOSS

Writing in *Computer Weekly*,[1] Charles Drayson, an IT partner at Andersen Legal, evaluates the problems of consequential loss – i.e. revenue lost or costs accrued as a result of system failure.

Unlike direct losses, such as the cost of replacing equipment damaged by misuse, consequential loss is open-ended and legally complex. For example, a consequential loss clause could enable a client to claim lost revenue due to system downtime based on total annual revenues, divided by 365, multiplied by the number of days the system is down. Alternatively, it could mean fines imposed by the government for non-compliance with new regulations are passed on to the outsourcer. A health services provider whose system goes down could be faced with huge legal action if patients die as a result.

In practice, consequential loss is by far the biggest exposure for a company choosing to outsource a business process – the cost of non-delivery is usually far greater than the cost of the technologies involved. The problem is that consequential loss is so difficult to quantify and can involve potentially huge sums of money. The actual liability will often depend on the outcome of complex legal cases. As such, suppliers will fight hard to avoid them.

So how do you resolve the conflict? Drayson advises two approaches:

☐ Negotiate to agree specific types of consequential loss that can be documented and described in the contract as direct loss.

☐ Agree to a cap on consequential loss claims.

BLG's Simon Shooter accepts the need for some form of cap but urges extreme caution:

⟨ A typical liability cap will limit the outsourcer's exposure to a maximum sum, or a maximum percentage of the total contract value. In practice, these clauses need very careful scrutiny. ⟩

[1] Charles Drayson, 'Don't Leave it All to the Lawyers', in *Computer Weekly*, 13 December 2001.

Shooter cites a contract that limits liability to $1.5 million. This sounds like a significant sum, but does the limit refer to the amount per claim, the maximum amount per year, or the total amount that will be accepted over the life of a ten-year contract? Clearly each is very different.

Liability can sometimes be capped by category, too, so that the maximum amount payable is restricted for each type of loss separately. Often, outsourcers will look to eliminate certain types of liability altogether. For example, many contracts will exclude consequential loss through loss of profit, goodwill or anticipated savings.

While the courts have the right to side with outsourcers if they believe their liquidated damages are punative, they can also overrule liability caps under the Unfair Contract Terms Act if they deem them unreasonable. An outsourcer that sets a liability cap at an unreasonably low level, or restricts the scope too far, is increasing the likelihood of the courts overruling it. If that happens, it effectively faces unlimited liability. It is therefore in everyone's interest to set a realistic cap.

Charles Drayson's article points out that the higher the risk on the outsourcer, the greater the degree of financial complexity, indemnity cost and opacity of the agreement. In other words, unlimited liability contracts will cost you more. Shooter is unconvinced.

> ‹ BLG advises that you should look with extreme care at the types of losses you might incur if a supplier defaults – and fight hard. For example, if loss of profit is your biggest risk, why on earth would you exclude it? ›

SUMMARY

1 Follow up supplier references in detail.

2 Draw up the contract so that the supplier cannot squeeze one area without impacting revenue elsewhere. Include a schedule of costs for as many different service options as possible, to limit the possibility of hidden additional charges emerging later.

3 Be very careful when writing penalties into the SLA. If not properly thought through, you can easily give outsourcers an incentive to do precisely the opposite of what you want.

4 Always have an exit strategy built into the contract. Should you need to hand over the contract, the incumbent has an incentive to obstruct the new outsourcer. Advance contractual planning is a must to prevent this from happening.

5 If you want to work in partnership with unions, make sure you pick an outsourcer which does not object to doing so.

6 Penalties written into the SLA should be pre-agreed at a reasonable level and take into account certain forces outside the supplier's control. If an outsourcer believes it is being unfairly penalized, it can take the matter to court.

7 It makes sense to base penalty levels around the same level as the supplier's margins: make your supplier squeak, not scream.

8 Outsourcers often press for caps on their liability when writing consequential loss provisions into a contract. If you agree, be sure you specify exactly how and to what these caps apply. But if loss of profit is your biggest risk, why exclude or limit it at all?

CHAPTER 22

SERVICE LEVEL AGREEMENTS

In a service level agreement (SLA), all three words carry equal importance. The document should define precisely what services are to be delivered and the levels of performance expected, but it must also be an agreement – not a unilateral declaration. It is important to recognize that a supplier will agree to virtually any level of virtually any service – *at a price*. It is far better to work with the supplier to agree a reasonable balance between requirements and cost.

The key to an SLA is to remember it is output-based. It should outline:

- ☐ What services are to be delivered.
- ☐ Where they should be delivered.
- ☐ By when.

For example, a contract may involve delivering new PCs to a desktop. It should identify:

- ☐ The metric to be applied (e.g. delivery time).
- ☐ A unit of measurement (e.g. days).
- ☐ Volume capability (e.g. we can deliver in X days, up to a maximum of 50 systems at any one time).
- ☐ A period over which the metric applies (e.g. penalties at three days and then daily).

It is essential that both parties understand that the SLA does not represent a set of targets – it sets out the absolute worst case. The target is perfection!

The unit of measurement needs careful consideration. Most people when writing SLAs tend to go for one month as an arbitrary timescale for delivery of a service. In fact, these things will vary depending on the type of user, length of business cycle (month, quarter, etc.) and other factors. Typically, in an IT outsource contract, there are four measures:

1 Availability – how many hours of outage over a given period.

2 Reliability – how many separate failures there are over a given period.

3 Serviceablity – how long it takes to fix an outage.

4 Response time – how long it takes from reporting a problem to resolution.

On top of these basic measures, conditions are then mutually agreed. These are likely to be volumetric, e.g. 'We can answer help-desk calls in three rings, but if we get more than 500 in a day, the response time may fall to six rings', or 'We will be able to close a call within two hours, but if the call is not properly authorized in advance of placement we cannot make that commitment'.

Thought must be given to the timescales applied to each measure. For example, availability agreements often set out a number of hours downtime for a given month. While it may be acceptable to go for 20 hours a month without a given service, if all 20 hours fell on the same day, it almost certainly would not.

David Strang at law firm BLG points out that it is very difficult to create legally enforceable metrics in an SLA that last over time, so all metrics need regular review. Given that most outsourcing contracts are designed to run for ten years, you would expect the nature of the contract to change enormously over that period. Businesses grow, shrink, acquire, dispose and merge. He advises clients to try to anticipate as many possible changes as possible up front, but at the same time recognize that the contract will need regular reviewing and updating. The goal is not to agree an annual contract review, but to put together an infrastructure whereby the contract can be continually refined.

DRAWING UP THE SLA

Service definitions and exceptions

Is it realistic to demand a sub-second response time for every transaction, for a given class of transaction, for one specific transaction, across all systems? This is critical as it comes back to price. As mentioned above, an outsourcing service provider will be able to meet virtually any condition you set, at a price. It is essential that you have identified the service you really need.

Bob Aylott at outsourcing consultancy Orbys thinks that the best approach is to set a generic service expectation, with specific tasks highlighted. For example, the system should respond to any transaction request within four seconds, but customer requests should receive sub-second responses.

It is common to identify lowest common denominator sets of transactions and group them into service element groups (SEGs). Careful thought should be given as to what should be included in each group. Again, making the groups too wide will drive up service costs unnecessarily.

Cost of quality

It is important to remember the golden rule of total quality management: high-quality service costs everyone less than low-quality service. If the system is built such that it does not go wrong, it does not need an expensive maintenance and support operation behind it. Aylott says you should therefore focus your negotiations around availability and argue that costs should not be higher as a result.

Penalties and compensation

'It is important to graduate these so that poor service never has a binary cost: the cost should always grow as the service deteriorates,' says Aylott. Remember the PC that took weeks to reach your desk once the three-day deadline had passed? A graduated penalty cost would ensure that by day four, the outsourcer was desperate to deliver the machine.

Service debits

As mentioned in Chapter 21, service credits are effectively penalties on the outsourcers, should they fail to meet a particular service level. Service debits are the reverse – a bonus payable if they over-perform on the service level targets.

All the advisors I have spoken to agree that service debits are pointless. Service levels are set based upon the business requirement – the call centre must answer the telephone within three rings, the PC must be fixed in four hours, the number of cheques processed over 10,000 per hour. Over-performance has no business benefit for the client – otherwise it would have set the threshold higher in the first place.

For an outsourcer, the service debit is simply a route to generating extra margin.

TIMING THE SERVICE LEVEL AGREEMENT

Building an outsourcing contract is a complex process. Large, multi-location contracts can take between six and nine months to negotiate. Throughout that time, the client has to maintain open dialogue with all the interested parties, keep the staff informed and ensure that all the stakeholders in the decision stay on board. Clearly the faster the deal can be concluded, the better for everybody.

At the same time, an outsourcer will be very reluctant to tie itself to an SLA until it has had the opportunity to experience running the contract for a while. Outsourcers will argue that the assumptions that they use to drive their service level commitments up to that stage will be based solely on client input. Some clients will provide extremely accurate data based upon extensive internal research; others will deliver widely over-estimated information, usually through lack of rigour rather than any intent to deceive. In these situations, once the contract begins, the fallout will always be unpleasant – the outsourcer will be missing all of its profitability targets, the client's internal customers will be receiving a service well below expectations, fingers will point; an inauspicious start.

Unisys's Guy Warren suggests that implementing an SLA on day one is a mistake:

> ❬ We would normally expect to discuss the basic service levels, sign the contract and then enter a period of "burn-in" where each party gets to understand exactly how the relationship will shape up and what reasonable expectations may be. At the end of the first three months, each party will have enough data to write a meaningful SLA. ❭

Sign a multi-year, multi-million-pound contract before the service levels have been agreed? Is this really safe? Robert Morgan, CEO of Morgan Chambers, Europe's largest outsourcing consultancy thinks not:

> ❬ Guy is right in that a detailed SLA takes time to develop as each party learns more about the other, but we would not recommend that a client contracts in a deal without some form of SLA in place. We normally suggest that a series of interim SLAs are developed to

bridge the gap. The client should expect a three-month SLA at the beginning of the contract with regular, iterative reviews over the first year to 18 months. **'**

Morgan suggests that the client should build a first-cut SLA, working with the internal customers and then taking it to the supplier to fine-tune. Understanding that this is an interim, time-bound document should set the supplier's mind at rest as it is not making expensive, long-term commitments.

The iterative SLA approach means that initial negotiation time is kept to a minimum while the client's interests are protected throughout.

SUMMARY

1   An SLA should define what services are to be delivered, where they should be delivered and by when. Each metric to be applied should specify a unit of measure, volume capability and period of application.

2   In IT outsourcing, measures typically include availability, reliability, serviceablity and response time, plus mutually agreed conditions.

3   Think carefully about the timescales applied to each measure. Twenty hours downtime a month may be acceptable, but what if it was all on the same day?

4   Anticipate as many changes upfront as possible, but recognize that an SLA will need continual refining.

5   Set generic service expectations and pinpoint specific tasks that need higher service levels. It is common to group sets of tasks into SEGs, but making them too broad can drive up costs.

6   Remember the golden rule of TQM – high-quality service costs everyone less than low-quality service.

7   Graduate penalties so that the cost to the outsourcer grows as the service deteriorates.

8   Service debits are pointless, except to boost the outsourcer's margins. Over-performance has no business benefit for the client.

9   Operate with a first-draft SLA, on the understanding that it will be refined once the outsourcer has had hands-on experience of the contract. This cuts negotiation time and protects your interests.

CHAPTER 23

INTELLECTUAL PROPERTY RIGHTS

In any long-term arrangement, irrespective of whether the client's goals are aligned with those of the outsourcer, there will always be one clear, strategic point of difference: the outsourcer will want to ensure it is as indispensable as possible to the client, in order to protect its long-term position. The client will, of course, have the opposite goal.

In the main, this factor is easily manageable, but it comes to the fore when discussing intellectual property rights (IPR) – defining who owns what knowledge.

Intellectual property falls into three categories:

- ☐ Client IPR.
- ☐ Outsourcer IPR.
- ☐ Third-party IPR.

Simon Shooter of law firm BLG is a specialist in this field and claims that the key to successful IPR negotiation is to aim for no surprises on either side.

CLIENT IPR

Identify and maintain your IPR throughout the contract. Much of the intellectual property will typically be tied up in systems and processes. Over time, both will change dramatically, to the extent that only a small fraction of original software code or process designs may remain unaltered at the end of a contract. If these processes and systems are critical to your business, you should ensure this does not affect your rights over the information.

Provide the supplier with an explicitly stated licence to use the systems or processes *only* in order to comply with their obligations under the contract and throughout any termination process.

If the supplier has modified software code, you need not only the right to the software, but also access to the source code. Often code is written by staff who, in the event that a contract ends, would transfer with that contract under TUPE (see Chapter 26) so, as long as access to the source code is secured, maintaining it may not be an issue.

Code is normally held in escrow – i.e. by an independent third party who is instructed to release it to the client when (and only when) a pre-agreed set of conditions is triggered.

According to Shooter, many of the disputes around IPR begin when an outsourcing contract rolls in an existing, lesser contract. For example, a client may have a supplier handling a project to refresh its entire estate of desktops. This agreement is stand-alone and relatively simple, often based on a standard contract. The client may then decide to outsource all of its IT requirements, including this component, and award the contract to the existing supplier. When the contract begins, the initial project may be rolled into it. Shooter's advice is stark:

> ‹ Do not do it. Always keep the contracts separate, otherwise the lack of rigour over IPR in the one project can undermine the integrity of the larger outsourcing contract. You should just ensure that the terms of the outsourcing contract specify that the deal is contingent on the initial project being successfully delivered. ›

OUTSOURCER IPR

Here the key really does lie with Shooter's 'no surprises' axiom. He advises that the client sets out its utopian desire – i.e. everything that, all things being equal, they want to own.

The key questions are:

☐ Is it a bespoke system or process?

☐ If so, do we want to own it?

☐ What is the cost increment for ownership versus licensing?

☐ What would the impact be of allowing it to be used by our competitors?

In IT terms, Shooter contends that most people worry too much about the IPR issue – very little IT IPR is truly transferable without a good deal of investment.

IPR and BPO

One area where supplier/client IPR has a critical role to play is in business processing outsourcing contracts, where an outsourcer takes over a client's operation altogether. Typically a client will expect that the operation of his business is his IPR. However, most BPO contracts are put together by the outsourcer, on the basis that they can bring dramatic process improvements to bear which will drive down cost and allow them to deliver an improved service and lower cost, and still derive a margin.

As a result, over time, the majority of the procedures will change to the outsourcer's own ways of doing things. As outsourcers grow their presence in the market, they will clearly be bringing in intellectual capital from their experience in other projects, and will often see that as their IPR. While the contract is running smoothly, this is clearly not an issue, but at contract termination time, or when some form of dispute arises, it can be a critical stumbling block.

This is sometimes quite clear cut. For example, a major IT outsourcer will inevitably have its own standard approach to software quality assurance. It would be unreasonable for a client to expect to claim that process as its own. Equally, where a third party is brought in to implement health and safety practices, the client should expect those practices to become its intellectual property at the end, just as it would in any other form of management consultancy engagement.

Ultimately, however, the only way to be sure is to specify exactly what constitutes client or supplier IPR.

The procedures manual

A good starting position is for the client to demand IPR for everything in the procedures manual. If there is anything that the outsourcer is not willing to hand over, it should be excluded from the manual. This has a number of benefits:

1   It clarifies who owns what up front.

2   It forces the supplier to state explicitly what it is not willing to hand over. This in turn means that the client has an opportunity to identify the gaps and start to build contingency plans to fill them in the event of contract termination.

For example, a distribution outsourcing provider is very unlikely to be willing to hand over IPR on its distribution systems, since these give it its core competitive edge. By identifying this fact early, the client can build in a contingency plan and factor in the time and cost impact of having to find another product and migrate data.

An alternative position that may be acceptable for both parties is for the outsourcer to own the IPR, but to allow the client to use the processes or software free of charge during the life of the contract, and then provide the right to purchase a license to use it following its termination. Again, disruption is minimized for the client and contingency costs can be calculated.

In these cases, it is clearly essential to have some kind of clause agreeing to reasonable pricing. Normally, this takes the form of a commitment to provide 'most favoured pricing' – a cost comparable to that paid by other customers. This ensures the outsourcer is not given an easy way to hike up prices in order to claw back revenue lost due to early termination.

Third-party equipment procurement

Ownership of third-party hardware will depend primarily on your financial objectives. If you are keen to keep as much as possible off your balance sheet, you will clearly want the outsourcer to buy everything and sell it back as an expense-line service. In practice, financial objectives can change over the lifetime of a contract, so it is a good idea to build in some flexibility.

Keeping the contract between the client and the equipment supplier is certainly the simplest option, but remember that the big, global outsourcers have enormous purchasing power. It is therefore sensible to look at the option of having the outsourcer act as a procurement agent, negotiating on your behalf. In some cases it can be sensible for both the outsourcer and client to work separately to try to find the best deal.

Alternatively, the outsourcer can buy the equipment on condition that, at contract termination, it will sell it to the client under pre-agreed terms.

With software, things are more complex. Many software suppliers will charge for a licence transfer from outsourcer to client, should the contract end.

THIRD-PARTY IPR

With third-party IPR, it is critical to understand what you will be able to take over, what you will have to pay to transfer and what will have to be bought from scratch. Shooter advises his clients to ask the outsourcer to provide the software on (as near as possible) a transferable, no-cost basis. The outsourcer will come back and make clear what can and cannot be done, and lay out costed options.

A fair and equitable approach

Shooter believes that it is important to acknowledge that you cannot demand everything for free. You need to recognize the outsourcer's right to its own IPR and be willing to discuss which elements are and are not negotiable. In this way, you will be able to make decisions about the value, relative to the cost, of each component.

SUMMARY

1   IPR for different components of a system or process can reside with client, outsourcer or third party. Aim for 'no surprises' by clarifying who owns what.

2   IPR may be tied up in systems and processes that change over the course of the contract. Ensure you have the rights to the modified software and access to the source code (which should normally be held in escrow).

3   Do not roll an existing contract into a larger outsourcing deal. Lack of rigour over IPR in the smaller contract can undermine the larger one.

4   For each bespoke component, consider whether you want to own it, the cost of ownership versus licensing, and the implications of allowing your competitors to use it.

5   In BPO deals, experienced outsourcers bring in intellectual capital from other projects which they see as their IPR. This can be a problem at contract termination time if client and supplier IPR are not clearly specified.

6   Demand IPR for everything in the procedures manual. Exclude anything which the outsourcer will not hand over. This clarifies who owns what and means that you can build in contingency plans in the event of contract termination.

7   Alternatively, you might let the outsourcer own the IPR if it allows you to use the processes or software free of charge and gives you the right to purchase a license (at a competitive price) to use them if the contract ends.

8   Objectives change, so build in some flexibility – for example, make it a condition that, at contract termination, the outsourcer sells you the kit under pre-agreed terms.

9   With third-party IPR, understand what you can take over, what you will have to pay to transfer and what will have to be bought from scratch. Ask the outsourcer to provide software on a transferable, no-cost basis.

10   Be fair and equitable – you cannot demand everything for free.

CHAPTER 24

GOVERNANCE

Bob Aylott of outsourcing consultancy Orbys defines the aim of governance as:

> ‹ Being satisfied that what is being done is what is wanted. ›

In a joint venture, this is achieved largely through the board of directors. However, in a traditional outsourcing relationship, governance needs to be more formal and structured.

It is clearly a two-way process. The supplier needs to be kept informed of changes, expected spikes in demand, business plans, new product launches, etc. By bringing this information to the outsourcer's notice, the client ensures any negative impact on the service is minimized.

MANAGEMENT OF THE CONTRACT

Day-to-day service management is no different to managing internal staff. There is a need for change meetings and daily reviews. Beyond this, the relationship will differ depending upon whether it is a straightforward outsourcing contract or a partnership.

Outsourcing contract

In the case of an outsourcing contract, the client will appoint a primary interface. This will normally be a service management team that sits within an outsourced function, or the operations team in the case of BPO. The outsourcer will appoint an equivalent team that sits within the account management operation.

There will be regular review meetings between the client service management team, the account management team and relevant users. At these meetings, the competitiveness and appropriateness of the deal will be reviewed. Meetings will be largely benchmark-based and, if run effectively, will drive changes to the contract as it evolves to ensure both sides are delivering/achieving what they need.

The partnership team

If it is a partnership, the outsourcer will also appoint a client agent to lead a partnership team, which should contain staff from both sides and operate separately from the account director. Effort and money will usually be expended to build this into a close-knit, 'bonded' group.

The behaviour of the partnership team will inevitably be more collaborative than that of the service management team which, as the name suggests, represents the interests of the client to its counterparts in the outsourcer – often very strongly.

The partnership team has to deliver the agreed added value for each party. At the partnership review meetings, the team will facilitate reviews with senior management from both parties.

Whichever approach is taken, changes to the contract should be incremental and take the form of additional schedules to be added to the original documentation. If the entire contract is being re-worked, it is a sign of deeper problems.

ANNUAL REVIEWS

Every year, the outsourcer and client should agree:

- [ ] What they value.
- [ ] What they need to help deliver on their goals.
- [ ] A statement of intent for adding value (aligned with client objectives).

Aylott advises: 'Say what you are trying to achieve in the next year and reward on the basis of value realized against those goals.'

For example, an outsourcer may promise that its proposal will increase the bank's stock value. The bank may respond with an offer to sell stock to the outsourcer at current rates (or perhaps discounted current rates) on an agreed future date. If the share price rises, the outsourcer makes money; if it falls, it can lose. Arguably, the bank's share price is largely outside the control of the outsourcer, but this risk factor is neutral – the bank's stock could rise or fall. The outsourcer is promising to tip the balance. This is a classic example of shared risk/reward based totally on business objectives.

A SPECIALIST ON THE BOARD?

Outsourcing consultancy Morgan Chambers argues that the role of 'director of sourcing' should be a main board position. Whether a specific role needs to be created is debatable, but sourcing should certainly be high on the boardroom agenda.

Decisions about outsourcing have to balance flexibility and a lower asset base against higher exposure to risks. The board needs to weigh up the benefits and risks of outsourcing business processes with business functions. Doing both can lead to complexity and conflict. For example, an organization may choose to outsource HR to one vendor, IT to another and the customer service business process to a third. The customer service operation will have its own processes, expectations and demands for IT and HR. The outsourcer may well have technology standards it insists on working with to ensure it can hit SLAs, and/or great strength in its unique recruitment and retention processes.

The key is not necessarily to put a dedicated resource on the board, but to ensure the range of sourcing options is clearly understood by the board and evaluated regularly. Books like this are a good place to start, but there are many expert services available from consultants such as Morgan Chambers and Orbys, as well as organizations like the Outsourcing Institute (www.outsourcing.com).

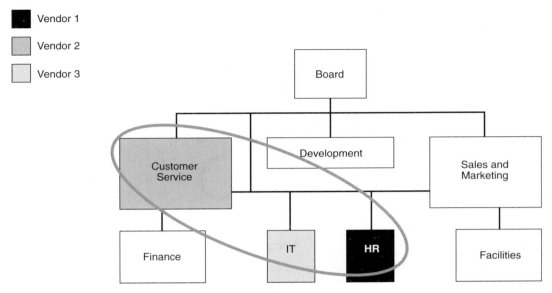

FIGURE 24.1: Conflict and complexity of multi-vendor outsourcing deals

SUMMARY

1 Governance in a joint venture is achieved largely through the board of directors, but in other outsourcing models it needs to be a formalized, two-way process between client and outsourcer.

2 The client is normally represented by a service management team in an outsourced function, or by the operations team in the case of BPO. The outsourcer appoints an equivalent account management team.

3 These teams will hold regular review meetings to ensure both sides are delivering/ achieving what is needed.

4 In a partnership, there should also be a close-knit, collaborative partnership team that includes staff from both sides and has to deliver the agreed added value for each party.

5 Any changes to the contract should take the form of additional schedules. A complete rewrite is a sign of deeper problems.

6 Hold in-depth annual reviews where you highlight goals for the following year and reward the outsourcer on the basis of value achieved against them.

7 Whether you need to appoint a sourcing specialist is a judgement call, but at least ensure the board clearly understands and regularly reviews the options.

CHAPTER 25

IT OUTSOURCING: SINGLE- OR MULTI-VENDOR?

As we saw in Chapter 20, one of the toughest decisions in IT outsourcing is whether to pick a single outsourcing partner, or to share the work across multiple, specialist suppliers. It is not a black-and-white decision – there are various options and combinations, and the choices you make will depend on your business priorities.

PROS AND CONS

Single-vendor outsourcing

The pros:

☐ Provides maximum accountability.

☐ Requires minimum amount of management overhead.

☐ High total contract value offers better opportunity for discounts.

☐ Model is attractive to outsourcers, who will bid aggressively for a contract.

☐ Can be the most cost-effective approach.

The cons:

☐ Difficult to break the relationship, which may be a source of strategic risk. (Multi-vendor relationships can keep suppliers on their toes.)

☐ Few suppliers are world-class in every respect. For example, the telcos tend to have best network management skills, and a maintenance business requires a very different management approach to, say, application development. Single-vendor outsourcing is therefore inappropriate if the motivation is to inject best-in-class skills.

Although it sounds simple, single-vendor outsourcing is very difficult to achieve. In practice, almost every IT operation outsources something already – there is usually an effective set of relationships in place for handling either desktop management or maintenance, help-desk or PC configuration, commodity supply or application development. Breaking effective processes in order to create a tidy, single-vendor contract may not be popular, easy or even desirable.

While single-vendor contracts can work out cheaper, there is a risk that over the life of the contract, the extra bargaining power which a single supplier carries can empower it to drive up margins over time, in ways that a mix of suppliers could prevent. It is therefore critical that single-vendor contracts are drawn up and managed carefully so as to protect against any abuse of position by the supplier.

Multi-vendor outsourcing

The pros:

☐ Best-of-breed. In a multi-vendor outsourcing environment, you should obtain the strongest skills and the best processes for each element of the service. (It is worth bearing in mind that best-of-breed is also used by some providers as an excuse for gaps in their portfolio. 'We believe that the customer should be free to choose the best-of-breed solution,' often translates as: 'We do not know how to deliver that service – you are on your own.')

☐ Incumbent suppliers. A multi-vendor environment enables you to continue to capitalize on those relationships that are already in place and working well.

The cons:

☐ Finger pointing. Multi-vendor implies multiple points of handover among the different suppliers. In putting together successful outsourcing contracts, multi-vendor environments will inevitably take longer, cost more and open up more opportunities for conflict and error.

☐ Complexity. Multiple suppliers need to be managed. Most or all will compete with one another in one or more areas. Turf wars are a common feature of contract management. With multi-vendor contracts, the management overhead can therefore be very high – possibly as high as with an in-house environment. This is problematic if you are looking for the process to deliver behavioural change in your own management team.

☐ Stifled innovation. An outsourcer that has a great business idea in a single-source contract has little to risk by proposing and implementing it – at worst, it improves the relationship, at best it generates new revenue. In a multi-vendor environment, however, there is always a risk of the idea being stolen by competitors. Multi-vendor environments can therefore never operate with the same level of trust and openness.

PRIME CONTRACTING

With prime contracting, the client has a single contract with an outsourcer, but the outsourcer subcontracts elements of the total service delivery to third parties of either its own, or the client's, choice. Prime contracting holds out the promise of the best of both worlds – the simplicity of a single-source relationship, with access to the best skills, yet without having to compromise incumbent relationships.

As with single source, outsourcers like prime-contractor relationships because they retain control of the relationship at the expense of their competitors. This means that deals are generally hard-won and aggressively priced.

On the downside, outsourcers have relatively few customers – even Computer Sciences Corporation (CSC), the third largest in the world, only operate 130 contracts worldwide. This means that they do not have the same flexibility as most other industries when it comes to balancing margins across multiple contracts. For an outsourcer, every contract has to meet all financial metrics, including percentage gross margin. With a prime-contractor arrangement, all services are invoiced through the single supplier. The outsourcer will therefore have to add a margin on every third-party item in order to protect its own margins and meet targets. As a result, prime-contracting will always cost more than multi-vendor outsourcing.

In response to demands for transparency, most outsourcers operate open-book pricing on all third-party items. This means that they commit to a maximum margin level that they will add to a given product and allow access to the original invoices and even full audit rights to the client, to prove that they are following the rules. This approach does, however, require careful review.

Many technology suppliers offer a co-operative marketing rebate to resellers of their systems or software. This rebate (sometimes referred to as 'soft dollar' in the reseller channel) is usually paid quarterly and in arrears. It will not appear on the invoices. While the cooperative marketing rebate is theoretically designed to help resellers stimulate demand for further sales, in practice it is often used to offset the tight margins associated with selling commodity technology. In other words, a technology supplier may make only a few points of margin on a given system at the time of sale but could receive another 3–5 per cent in the form of a retrospective rebate.

ALLIANCES

In 1996, JP Morgan took a more radical approach to IT outsourcing. Simon Knowles, CSC's European director of marketing for new business development, takes up the story:

‹ Peter Miller, CIO at JP Morgan, understood the pros and cons of each approach when he set out to implement an outsourcing contract. Instead, he opted to challenge prospective suppliers to put together consortia that would give him the benefits of a multi-vendor approach, with the control and behaviours of a single-source deal. The winning bid came from the Pinnacle Alliance – a consortium led by CSC and including Andersen Consulting (now Accenture), AT&T Solutions and BANI. CSC is in charge of the overall contract, Accenture handles application development, AT&T the voice and data networks and BANI desktop and LAN management in the US. Pinnacle Alliance offered the best mix of strengths and skills. ›

The Pinnacle Alliance is not a legal entity, but a group with its own executive committee that sets strategic direction. Each supplier (as well as JP Morgan), is represented on the committee, which is led by a CSC executive. JP Morgan's relationship is with the Alliance, not with CSC. As one might expect in an IT outsourcing contract, there are penalties and rewards based upon performance. These are shared equally among the partners. The performance metrics are similar to those in any other contract.

How well has the Alliance worked? Six years on, it is still going strong and JP Morgan seems pleased with progress. In 1998, market analyst Dataquest ran a short study on the process in which it stated: 'Peter Miller, CIO of JP Morgan, believes the focus on day-to-day IT operations and planning is still taking precedence over future IT strategy and direction.' Over time, Mr Miller's expectation was that the JP Morgan management team would be able to shift their focus onto strategy, but the complexity of the arrangement meant that it was always going to take time and effort to bed down.

The Pinnacle Alliance appears to have achieved most of the objectives that JP Morgan had from the outset, but it is worth noting that I can find no examples of this approach being copied or adopted elsewhere.

SUMMARY

1   In IT outsourcing, the choice to go with a single source or multiple suppliers will depend on your business priorities.

2   Single-vendor outsourcing has the advantages of maximum accountability, minimum management overheads and more competitive pricing.

3   The cons are that it is hard to break the relationship; few suppliers are world-class in every respect, and existing contracts make single-source outsourcing very difficult to achieve in practice.

4   There is also a risk of a single supplier driving up margins over time; contracts should be drawn up to protect against any such abuse.

5   The multi-vendor approach allows you to select best-of-breed skills and processes for each component of the service, as well as capitalize on existing relationships that are working well.

6   However, a multi-vendor contract can also result in excess complexity, duplication of resources, finger pointing and stifled innovation as suppliers strive to protect their competitive interests.

7   Prime contracting offers the best of both worlds by using a single supplier to manage existing contractor relationships. However, the prime contractor needs to add margin to third-party services. While acceptable margins can be agreed, time-consuming review procedures are required to maintain transparency.

8   JP Morgan tried the novel approach of asking consortia of suppliers to bid for its IT outsourcing contract. The resulting deal with the CSC-led Pinnacle Alliance has been reasonably successful, but the approach has so far failed to catch on.

CHAPTER 26

THE ACQUIRED RIGHTS DIRECTIVE (TUPE)

TUPE stands for Transfer of Undertakings (Protection of Employment), and refers to the regulations that govern the transfer of staff in any potential outsourcing arrangement. TUPE is actually the UK enactment of European law known as Council Directive 2001/23/EC. Similar laws have been enacted in other EC member countries. Originally it was known as the Acquired Rights Directive, which was put in place in 1977; the UK then implemented TUPE legislation in 1981. In 2001, European legislation refined the terminology and allowed member states to bring pensions into scope. The UK is expected to implement this new legislation in 2002.

According to the legislation, an 'undertaking' is any sufficiently stable and identifiable business function or process. This applies to most outsourcing situations – which means so does TUPE. Size is not a limiting factor; TUPE covers anything from one person to many thousands, and any kind of activity, whether public or private sector.

There are basically two types of TUPE situation:

1 A function is outsourced for the first time to a third party, which is relatively straightforward.

2 A further transfer takes place, from one third party to another. There is no limit on the number of future transfers to which TUPE applies – if a further transfer were to take place at any time, then the TUPE rules would still have to be followed.

THE BASICS

The aim of TUPE is to ensure employees involved in the undertaking do not lose their jobs as a result of the transfer and that there is no variation in their terms and conditions. If any dismissal takes place, it would automatically be considered unfair.

Aspects such as pay and working hours are obviously covered, but the directive goes much further than that. For example, if an employee of an IT department who receives his annual salary review in August is transferred to an outsourcer which carries out its reviews in April, no change can be made – the employee's review date must remain in August indefinitely. It is not possible for a company to vary the conditions of employment even if the employee agrees, and even if the company offers to 'buy out' terms and conditions in order to harmonize workforce arrangements. Collective agreements with unions are also transferred, as are existing liabilities such as personal injury claims.

TUPE can cover:

- ☐ Pay and bonuses.
- ☐ Working hours.
- ☐ Union agreements.
- ☐ Location.
- ☐ Holiday entitlements.
- ☐ Redundancy terms.
- ☐ Annual reviews.
- ☐ Personal injury claims.
- ☐ Unfair dismissal claims.

If there is any doubt in the matter, it is safest to assume that TUPE applies. In fact, the laws are gradually being changed (and UK case law reflects this) to give a presumption that TUPE is relevant. It would then be up to a company to prove that it did not apply.

So why would anyone want to argue that? An organization about to outsource might try to show TUPE is not relevant because this could mean a cheaper contract, since no financial allowance would be needed to cover the cost of enforcement. But if the client asserts that TUPE does not apply, you can expect the outsourcer to seek an indemnity to protect it in any subsequent claims, should the courts rule against it. The provider is likely to look very closely at this area as part of the due diligence process. It will need to know all about the staff's contractual arrangements, because these could be significantly different to (and potentially more expensive than) its standard terms and conditions. If there are likely to be redundancies following the agreement, the outsourcer will want to know all about the client's redundancy packages, because these will of course apply. Collective agreements with unions will also continue to apply, along with existing holiday allowances, bonus entitlements and pay arrangements.

This area can become murky when second-generation transfers occur, when the question of who gives the indemnity will need to be negotiated. Normally, such an indemnity will run for a limited period, so anyone taking over the contract will look to balance costs and risks. The second company will be looking to offer competitive terms and conditions, and to provide the function at a lower cost by employing fewer staff.

From mid-2002, TUPE may well also apply to pension arrangements, depending on when and if the UK legislation is enacted. Previously pensions were not covered, so for staff the effect was as if they had taken up a new job. This was a significant point in negotiations with unions and staff associations, and many companies chose to carry over existing pension arrangements to preserve the goodwill of employees – and protect themselves from the adverse impact of potential public disputes.

When TUPE does not apply

For TUPE to apply, you have to have a transfer, and you have to have an undertaking. There is no rigid definition of either term. A transfer could be of intellectual property, assets, goodwill or contracts and not necessarily of people. However, if an organization tries to avoid TUPE by not transferring employees, in any subsequent claim the courts will look very closely at the situation. Cases can – and do – go either way. If you know you have an inefficient business department and you are looking to outsource it, you cannot make people redundant purely to make the outsourcing proposal more attractive to a supplier. On the other hand, any organization is entitled to restructure and there is a need for balance and compromise. TUPE would not apply if the new activity was not sufficiently similar to the old one. This could be the case where a company closes a department and decides to make occasional use of an external service. Again, any services arrangement could be subject to scrutiny if there was a claim.

After the transfer

What if the activity is restructured after the transfer? What if transferred employees are subsequently put on to other projects, far removed from their original work? It is certainly more than possible for this to happen and TUPE would not prevent it – but the rules will still apply.

It could be argued that TUPE tends to prevent fair competition. The law is far from rigid and there is a certain ebb and flow in decision-making. Currently there are certain moves to limit and define exactly what constitutes a TUPE situation. But, in summary, it is always safest to presume that the regulations apply and plan accordingly.

FORTHCOMING CHANGES TO TUPE

The following is taken verbatim (with permission) from an April 2002 memorandum, issued by Unisys's Office of the General Counsel to internal staff:

‘There have been a number of interesting judgements in this area. However, the state of the European and domestic law on the issues of what constitutes "an undertaking" and "a transfer" remains unsatisfactory.

A recent judgment by the Employment Appeal Tribunal (*Rossiter versus Pendragon plc*) further complicated the question in relation to the new employer's rights to vary conditions of employment of transferred employees after the transfer. Since *obiter* remarks by Lord Slynn in the House of Lords judgment in the *Wilson* and *Meade* cases, the prevailing view is that any such variations, which are made *due to the transfer* are ineffective, even if the employee consents to them. However, the employer may still vary the contract on a consensual basis, if the reason for that variation is not the transfer. Harmonization of employment terms is likely to be considered as "due to the transfer", and therefore ineffective. It remains a complete mystery as to how and when the link with the transfer can be broken.

In the *Rossiter* case, an employee resigned claiming constructive dismissal some 16 months after being transferred under TUPE, complaining that the new employer had altered his commission and holiday arrangements and had reduced his responsibilities. In the first instance the Tribunal refused his claim on the grounds that he had affirmed his contract by working for 16 months under his new conditions, and therefore it was no longer open to the employee to accept the "repudiatory" breach of the employer (if there was one) and claim constructive dismissal. The Employment Appeal Tribunal (EAT) said that the Tribunal had erred in law and the usual "contractual" constructive dismissal tests did not apply if the change in working conditions was due to a TUPE transfer. The EAT stated that where employees are subjected to a detriment following a transfer, the right to claim constructive dismissal may arise even where the changes introduced by the new employer do not amount to a breach of the employee's contract. This decision suggests that employers who acquire staff as a result of a TUPE transfer may be liable for unfair dismissal if they alter transferred employees' benefits and/or conditions even when such benefits and/or conditions are of a non-contractual nature (e.g. non-guaranteed overtime, discretionary benefits, etc.).

The UK Government has started a consultation process with a view of amending the existing TUPE regulations. The process is due to finish in December this year. The proposed amendments are intended to increase certainty in this area. These include:

☐ Special rules on transfers within public administration.

☐ "Presumption" of transfer in service contracting-out and outsourcing arrangements.

☐ Transfer of occupational pension rights to the new employer.

☐ Obligation on the part of the transferor to notify the transferee of all the rights and obligations with regard to the employees that are to be transferred.

☐ Amendments to the regulation allowing dismissal of the transferred employees for economical, technical or organizational reasons.

☐ A new provision allowing the transferee to change terms and conditions of employment of the transferred employees for economic, technical or organizational reasons entailing changes in the workforce.

☐ A new provision that requires the transferee to continue to recognize the recognition declaration made by Central Arbitration Committee under the provision of the Employment Relation Act 1999. ›

SUMMARY

1 Transfer of Undertakings (Protection of Employment), or TUPE, regulations apply in most outsourcing situations, irrespective of the type of activity or number of staff transferred. They also continue to apply to any further transfers of a contract.

2 The regulations forbid any changes to outsourced staff's pay, entitlements, terms and conditions, union arrangements and so on.

3 An organization might try to show that TUPE is not relevant in order to secure a cheaper contract, but the provider will examine the area closely.

4 Legislation is expected in 2002 to extend TUPE to pension arrangements, but many outsourcers already carry these across to avoid potential disputes.

5 In rare cases, you may be able to argue that TUPE does not apply, but the decision can be finely balanced and, in the event of a claim, any service arrangement could be subject to close scrutiny. If in doubt, assume that TUPE applies.

6 Proposed future changes to the directive should see the introduction of far more clarity and flexibility.

CHAPTER 27

INTERNAL POLITICS

In the late 1990s, Dave Claridge, a principal consultant at KPMG and highly experienced outsourcing advisor, was presented with his biggest challenge yet – a consulting engagement in the world of politics.

'A major European political party was having serious concerns about its membership administration. I wanted to boost intake, increase renewal rates and improve the service offered to existing members. The party also needed the new solution delivered extremely quickly for use in its election campaign. With the election less than two years away, the race was on.'

Claridge was involved in the entire process:

☐ Deciding whether improvements could be achieved internally or whether outsourcing was a viable alternative.

☐ Helping evaluate potential suppliers.

☐ Helping the party take the decision to outsource.

☐ Managing the transition to a steady state with the nominated outsourcing supplier.

In this case, the biggest challenge by far was – appropriately for a political party – the internal political landscape. Not only did the decision need the support of the entire party executive, but the internal membership administration staff also had to be convinced. All discussions had to be held with extreme sensitivity and confidentiality, and it was essential to show that any decision on outsourcing was based on rock-solid factual information, taking into account all of the risks and the diverse views of the various parties involved.

THE ANALYSIS PROCESS

Claridge applied a standard KPMG process – the 'People, Process, Technology review'. This enabled KPMG and the party to analyze working practices and identify ways to improve in an unemotional, strictly factual manner. The feedback demonstrated to the project sponsor that outsourcing was the best way to go. The next challenge was convincing the rest of the executive.

The process identified that the functionality needed to improve results would only be found in a system based on customer relationship management (CRM) principles, not a pure membership administration system as was in use at the time. In other words, there was a technical catalyst required as well as a change in working process.

Next, it identified the need for a telephone-based, direct-debit system. This would enable members whose subscriptions were coming to an end to approve a direct debit easily and ensure renewal was automatic from that point onwards. The old system relied on a cumbersome approach where direct debits were posted out to the member, filled in and shipped back for processing. This was shown to be a barrier to action by even the most loyal of members.

Claridge was asked to present the rationale for outsourcing at a meeting of the entire party executive. This was a daunting and difficult presentation in a highly charged political environment with wide-ranging views on the risks involved and the appropriateness of outsourcing – practically, emotionally and politically. Moreover, the issue of membership processing is considered by many to be at the core of the party.

By setting the importance of improving service to the membership against the risks and issues involved, Claridge was able to help the executive to take the decision to make the switch to outsourced membership processing. In the meantime, he set about ensuring that the party found the right supplier to deliver the service.

THE SERVICE

First, he made sure the contract incentivized the right supplier behaviours. The contract was structured with a minimum service price for delivering the functionality and service levels agreed. The service price was then staged with higher payments to the partner, which grew based upon the total number of members on the database. Service credits were also used in the contract as a mechanism to encourage the supplier to meet service levels and apply reductions in the service price if these were not met. Throughout, the key principle of the contract was to create a win-win situation for party and supplier.

Next, Claridge focused on the cultural fit. 'In most outsourcing environments, but particularly this one, cultural fit is the key. Unfortunately there is not that much quantitative evaluation that can be applied here – it is much more about feel, research and knowledge.'

He asked the outsourcer a set of questions:

- ☐ How do you treat your staff?
- ☐ What is your staff turnover?
- ☐ How do you engage with unions?
- ☐ What is your security policy?
- ☐ Who else do you work for?

Clearly the party did not want to engage with a company which worked closely with other, politically inappropriate clients, whether public or private sector. It would also be poor judgement to engage with a company that had a track record of making a large number of people redundant.

There were five or six serious bidders and these were quickly whittled down to two by structured negotiations. Some suppliers bid existing systems that they were already operating for other clients, with minor changes made to fit the new requirement. We felt this situation was sufficiently different that it would need a bespoke solution. Other suppliers offered services built around a Siebel CRM solution. Siebel as a CRM market-leader would certainly be capable of delivering, but in this case the budget available could not warrant the likely costs for both technology and implementation. In the end, we went with a tier-one supplier that had an affordable CRM solution with the appropriate functionality needed, a sound commercial arrangement and a good cultural fit.

It did take a number of months for the service to settle down, but this was no surprise given the extent of the changes that were needed – structurally, technically and culturally. In truth, the successful supplier had probably underestimated the complexity of the task and had to re-adjust its resource provision in the first few months. I am now quite confident the new approach has delivered what the party needed. *

Of course, it is not just political parties that have to face issues of internal politics when proposing to outsource a function or process. There are conflicting voices within every organization, and the radical nature of outsourcing is bound to produce some equally radical dissent.

The best advice for overcoming such political opposition is to do as Claridge did and make sure your analysis is always thorough and methodical, your rationale factual and unemotional. Following some sort of formal process can be useful in these situations, although you should also find time to openly and frankly address people's individual questions and concerns. A good business case should speak for itself, and if an organization is too busy with political infighting to hear it, then it has little chance of success anyway.

SUMMARY

Internal politics is inevitable and should be combated with fact, reason and thoroughness. A good business case speaks for itself.

CHAPTER 28

EXIT STRATEGIES

The UK spent a total of $8 billion on outsourcing in 2001. Yet according to research by D&B,[1] 25 per cent of outsourcing contracts break down every year and an extraordinary 50 per cent fail in the first five years.

Simon Shooter, a partner at law firm BLG and a specialist in outsourcing, says:

> Outsourcing arrangements are normally built on a spirit of friendship and cooperation and it is very easy to assume this spirit will prevail. In practice, with a ten-year contract, it is unlikely any of the original players will still be involved at the end.
>
> The short answer is to ensure there is clarity at the start – the outsourcing equivalent of a pre-nuptial agreement. It is not, however, enough to agree a termination agreement upfront and then lock it away until it is needed. The agreement should be subject to the same regular review as the rest of the outsourcing contract – if it does not reflect the current situation it will be largely valueless.
>
> Should the contract transfer to another vendor, the issue of handover should be well understood. Migrating services is going to mean stopping what you are doing and having someone else take over. The key here is to ensure it is handed over with minimum disruption.

Shooter advises the following, four-step process:

1 Identify the critical elements of the service, where levels of performance simply cannot be allowed to fall. These should be the focal point of any exit agreement.

2 Agree a handover process. Pulling a plug and flicking a switch is unlikely to be the lowest-risk approach. Normally there will be a degree of ramp-down/ramp-up.

3 Agree the service-level commitments and credits and the way in which they will be applied during ramp-down – it is probably unreasonable to expect an outsourcer to maintain the same service levels during this period. Shooter points out that this will almost certainly need to be renegotiated again at the time.

4 Address the question of supplier confidentiality, which is a challenging area. At the point of handover, you need the outsourcer to pass on the processes and policies it is currently

[1] Dun & Bradstreet research, 'Barometer of Global Outsourcing' 2000.

using on your behalf. Many of these may be seen by the service provider as a source of competitive advantage. It may not, for example, want its competition to know how it has managed to build such an efficient cost base.

ASPECTS TO CONSIDER

Termination assistance

The next focal point is termination assistance. This is a contractual commitment from the outsourcer to spend an agreed period helping the client through the process. According to Shooter, most clients (or their lawyers) underestimate how long that period needs to be. Lawyers tend to think 60 days is sufficient, and this is commonly set as the standard length of time over which the outsourcer must provide termination support. Anyone who has been through the process of supplier selection, short-listing, due diligence and implementation will know that a complex outsourcing arrangement can easily take nine months. Shooter advises the duration should be set by the CIO (in the case of IT outsourcing) or head of operations (in a BPO contract). Within the termination agreement, there should be a commitment by the outsourcer to assist in supplier selection – for example, by helping to estimate the number of people likely to be required or whether the assumptions being made are reasonable.

Transfer of equipment and technology

The next issue is around transfer of equipment and technologies. It should be established upfront what is to be transferred and the basis upon which prices will be set. Again, it is essential to ensure you have legislated for software licenses and maintenance contracts – often the biggest source of unpleasant surprises when a client changes provider.

When transferring data, you must also consider to whom the operational manuals belong. If information is held within them, do they belong exclusively to one party? Operating manuals are sensitive data for both the outsourcer and the client, so ownership should be clarified. Shooter advises that co-mingling of data should be avoided (i.e. what is mine is mine and should be kept separate from what is yours).

Dress rehearsals

Some organizations recommend the occasional 'dress rehearsal' for contract termination – something Shooter strongly advises against. 'They are complex, hugely expensive, and frankly demoralizing for all concerned. While it is prudent to plan for a breakdown in a relationship, it can be positively damaging to practise it,' he says.

Cost of termination

Who should pay for termination assistance? Shooter believes it depends on the reason for termination. If the outsourcer is in breach of contract then it is reasonable to expect it to pick up the costs, but if termination is for the convenience of the client, it is only fair and equitable that it shoulder the costs. In deadlock, costs may be split, but inevitably some negotiation will be needed.

Stranded costs

Commonly in an outsourcing arrangement, especially with IT, outsourcers will invest heavily upfront in the contract to gain efficiency savings that can be earned back over the life of the contract. The client receives technology upgrades that would otherwise have needed substantial capital costs and the outsourcer amortizes the cost over the duration of the contract. In the event that the contract is terminated early, the outsourcer will look to recover its costs. It is possible to negotiate such that the outsourcer is responsible for all this risk, but as discussed earlier, all supplier risk translates into contract cost in some way.

WHEN OUTSOURCERS GO BUST

If you are dependent on an outsourcer and it hits unexpected business problems, you have a major problem. Moving services back in-house is very difficult, so the best chance is probably to migrate to another third-party service provider. The problem with this situation is that there is no room for implementing the exit strategy so handover is going to be very difficult.

Fortunately, most companies enter a period of administration before they are formally wound down, especially complex businesses like outsourcers. The key is not to throw in the towel. Make contact with the administrators and work on a programmatic approach. Clearly things will not go all your own way, but there may be an opportunity to negotiate through the situation. If the company is folding, it may be more amenable to releasing IPR which will enable a new provider to take over the old processes more readily.

Shooter advises that you always include a clause in the contract to allow immediate termination if the outsourcer's business becomes financially unviable. This at least gives you the ability to move fast if the situation arises.

SUMMARY

1 Any long-term relationship risks breaking down at some point, so having a viable exit strategy in place from the beginning is vital – as are regular reviews of that process.

2 Focus on critical elements of the service, agree a handover process, decide what service-level commitments will be applied during ramp-down and address any supplier confidentiality issues that may arise.

3 Do not underestimate the length of the period over which the supplier will be needed to provide termination assistance. Nine months is not uncommon.

4 Establish how prices will be set when transferring equipment and technology. Do not forget software licences, maintenance contracts and operations manuals.

5 Avoid dress rehearsals – they are costly, complex and morale-sapping.

6 Decide who pays for termination assistance and under what circumstances.

7 If you want the outsourcer to shoulder all the risk of its upfront investment, expect to pay a higher contract price.

8 Handovers are difficult if the outsourcer goes bust. You may gain certain advantages by working with administrators, but include a clause in the contract that allows for immediate termination in the event of the outsourcer's collapse.

CHAPTER 29

CHOOSING AN IT SECURITY SUPPLIER

What should you ask a security service provider? Ray Stanton, director of the Security Centre of Excellence at Unisys and a ten-year veteran of IT security projects, identifies the following nine questions:

1 We need 24–7 service. Can you provide all the people, technology and skills to guarantee it?

2 What is the back-end support for your on-site people? Is there some form of nerve centre that tracks virus trends, known problems, etc.?

3 Are you BS7799 compliant? If not, are you compliant with any other recognized standards? No standards compliance, no deal.

4 What are your response times when an incident occurs?

5 What do you do following an incident report?

6 How do you garner global intelligence? The Nimda virus hit in Australia 12 hours before Western Europe – how would you capitalize on that 12-hour lead?

7 How do you protect yourself?

8 How will you maintain the level of skills of the people you will be bringing in or TUPE'ing across? Can we audit those skills directly or via a third party?

9 How do you vet new people coming in?

Any IT security provider worth its salt should be able to provide satisfactory answers to all of these questions without difficulty. If it cannot, avoid it.

Security outsourcers also need an exit strategy built into the contract. The principles are common to other outsourcing contracts, but standards compliance makes things very much easier. BS7799 lays out processes to be applied for effective security. The standard can therefore also be used in reverse to disengage. If there are no standards in place, disengagement is a lot more difficult.

CHAPTER 30

OUTSOURCING PEOPLE: STEPHANIE'S DIARY

Note: Stephanie's story is clearly a fictitious account, but it is based on feedback from HR directors, outsourcing specialists and a short survey of actual outsourced staff. Many thanks go to the real Stephanie – Stephanie Richards – who provided much of the research-based input for this piece.

Wednesday, 12 March 2000

Overslept again – when will the kids spend a whole night in their own bed without dragging me out of mine? When I arrived at work, we were all called into a meeting room where the team leaders announced that we were going to be outsourced.

Ten minutes later, rumours were flying around the office and there was non-stop huddling at desks, in the kitchen, at the photocopier . . . I suppose it's the fear of the unknown. I certainly feel very vulnerable – I really need this job, and finding another with the same flexitime will be almost impossible.

I telephoned Dave at work to tell him about it and he asked me how many were being made redundant. I just don't know and nobody could give me any answers. I felt sick and angry – I've been working hard for this company for seven years now and suddenly I feel like a spare part, being moved on without a second thought. What about my friends that I've worked with for the past seven years? I suppose, like most people, the thing I like best about my job is the people – they feel like a second family. Now some strangers want to come in and split us apart.

Nobody did much work today. Why should we care about our work if the company doesn't care about us? Janine tried to keep us positive, but she couldn't answer any of our questions so how could we be expected to believe her?

Went to bed with a splitting headache. If the kids make a fuss tonight, it's Dave that will be getting up for a change.

Thursday, 13 March 2000

Not much of a night's sleep, even though Dave did his bit.

I think after the initial shock of yesterday's announcement, we realized something was bound to change soon anyway – either shutdowns, redundancies or outsourcing. It's happened in a lot of companies like ours. Dave thinks I've always done a good job and been given glowing appraisals so I should be safe – whoever takes over, someone's got to do the work. To be honest, as long as I'm paid and don't lose flexitime, I can put up with most things. I do this job for the money, not for the fun of it.

Some of the team are more worried than I am, and I feel torn between believing what the doom-mongers are saying and trusting Dave's reassurances. I'd like to believe him, but the guys in the office keep coming up with new horror stories about outsourcers, redundancies and shutdowns – especially Steve. We all have loans, mortgages and pensions to worry about and we all need to work.

If we'd been given all the facts yesterday, however bad, at least we could have stopped worrying and started doing something. Now we are all hanging around waiting to see what happens. The office is like Death Row.

We are supposed to have a presentation tomorrow about the new outsourcing people and they've promised a question-and-answer session at the end. There are going to be confidential boxes for questionnaires, too, which I like – I can ask some of the awkward stuff without having to be a martyr in front of the rest of the team.

Friday, 14 March 2000

What a relief! This morning, they told me I'm keeping my job. Dave was right, though – with my good news came bad news for others. 'Bitter-sweet' comes to mind. They have decided to shut down the Manchester site and 15 jobs are going from my department. This was a big shock and I'm still very upset – Steve, Mary and Michelle are all going, as well as Jenny who is supposed to be getting married in July, poor girl. It was really awkward trying to console them when I knew my job was safe – I felt very guilty even though it wasn't my fault. After all these years of working and lunching together I just couldn't find the right words. In the end, I even felt I had to avoid people because nothing I could think to say would have helped. I never thought of myself as a callous person before.

Later on, I had the opportunity to see the roadshow because the new outsourcing company is touring. It actually sounds quite exciting now. I'm even beginning to look forward to the move. I also had a strange sense of pride – we must be valued employees and good at what we do otherwise the new company would not be so eager to take us on. This may not be so bad after all – only time will tell.

Cracked open a bottle of wine when I got through the door. What a day! I've never felt more exhausted in my life.

Friday, 20 April 2000

Tonight is party night. The outsourcer has arranged a welcoming party for all the staff moving to the new company – free food and alcohol, which has definitely warmed me to the place! I know its going to feel strange for a while, with the new people in and Mary and Michelle gone, but I keep reminding myself, I am only here for the money, so I may as well make the best of a new start.

Monday, 23 April 2000

Today was a bit of an anticlimax. I am still in the same office, doing the same job, only now it's with a hangover. It was a very smooth handover – in fact the only thing that's changed is the name above the door and the logo on my coffee mug. At least Janine is still my team leader and all the managers are staying put – no new flashy 'suits' to have to win over.

Although I know outsourcing is all about cutting costs and becoming more efficient, it's no fun when it affects your friends. To be honest, I am livid with my old company – it could have made the redundancies itself but it didn't have the courtesy or courage so it brought in an outsider to do its dirty work. If it had been better at getting rid of people who were not pulling their weight and managed things properly, we would not have got into such a mess that we had to be bailed out by the outsourcers.

So there it is – same job, same boss, some friends gone and a new sign on the door. Is that all there is?

Monday, 7 July 2000

Three months into the new company, things are going reasonably well. The workload has definitely gone up, but it is a bit more interesting because we are now much more aware of the value of the work we do. The first time Mr Higgins phoned me up for one of his special reports and I told him I couldn't do it without a purchase order, he was livid! I knew I was right though – we are only allowed to deliver a standard service now without charging extra. He shouted at Janine about me, but she backed me all the way. After years of putting up with the pompous old duffer, it's great to be in control – that will teach him and his management cronies to sell us off to another company like a bunch of old photocopiers.

Thank goodness they haven't changed my working hours. I can still collect the children from school and take Fridays off work to go down and look after Dave's mum.

The old employer has been absolutely useless. Once it had washed its hands of us it seemed to lose all interest, but the new company seems really nice – especially the HR people.

Monday, 30 October 2000

You'll never believe it, but I've signed up for the lifelong learning plan – a series of classes to help develop my IT skills, and the new people are paying for it all. Look out Bill Gates!

It transpires I had no need to worry about the safety net with the contract, or any of the terms and conditions. I'm on exactly the same deal as before. It's taken a while to clarify that, but I like the fact that the head-office people come up here regularly and take time to run though all this stuff with us.

Monday, 30 July 2001

Arrived at work to find out that the teething problems with the pension scheme have not been sorted out. We were originally told we wouldn't be worse off, but it turns out that we are. We are reassured it is now 'top priority', but that sounds a bit like 'the cheque's in the post' to me.

Despite the pension stuff, though, I think I have come out of this new arrangement pretty well. My new company looks after me better, takes more interest and has given me a lot more training opportunities. I just think they respect me for what I do instead of seeing me as a liability to be dealt with.

Our first salary review with the company seemed quite promising. Even though I am still on the same wage as before, there's now an incentive scheme. Who knows if it will ever turn into real money, but I like the idea of being paid on customer satisfaction and profitability – it makes me feel as though I will see some return from all the effort I put into my job. The old company would not have dreamed of that – they'd rather the money went to the shareholders or the bosses.

CHAPTER 31

OUTSOURCING PEOPLE: GETTING IT RIGHT

STEPHANIE'S STORY EXPLAINED

Stephanie's experiences are fairly typical of any outsourced employee who survives the transition. Outsourcing is a time when old certainties are suddenly challenged and loyalties tested. Apart from the obvious moral issues around responsibility for former employees, however, why should the company really care about all this touchy-feely stuff? The short answer is, survival.

Quality of service

Shifting employees over to someone else's headcount does not make them entirely someone else's problem. You are still reliant upon them to deliver the service to your business. One disgruntled ex-employee can do untold damage to your business – imagine what an entire operation could do. If an outsourcing project is to be successful, the staff have to be brought along with the entire process. With a high likelihood of redundancies along the way, this is far from straightforward.

Unique knowledge

Inevitably, any number of critical elements to each key process will be undocumented, living in the realm of 'how it really works' as opposed to the documented processes captured in the ISO9000 book. Losing long-term operational staff causes disruption as the remaining people struggle to fill the knowledge gaps. While these issues are rarely catastrophic, they do lead to inefficiencies, errors and further dissatisfaction among employees.

Many managers lose sight of the fact that clerical jobs are not the same as unskilled jobs. Bringing in graduate staff from outside to take over on the principle that 'they are smart so they will pick it up quickly' is seldom an effective strategy:

☐ They need to learn from the experienced staff over time.

☐ They are unlikely to stick around in a clerical job for very long once they have mastered the tasks.

☐ Competition for graduate employees means they are probably paid more than the long-term clerical staff they are replacing.

Security

Staff who leave the company carrying a grudge can do a great deal of harm. With a strong network of friends on the inside, a far better understanding of the systems than any of the management and a long list of system passwords and privileges, the opportunity for mischief is considerable.

Impact on the rest of the organization

If staff are unhappy, word will inevitably reach the staff in the rest of the business and rumours will fly – 'Who is next for the chop?', 'Have you heard what they have done to the XYZ department?' and so on.

It is important to inform the rest of the staff about the outsourcing of their colleagues, and to explain the reasoning behind the move and the process being followed. You should also update them with progress from time to time. The only effective counter to rumour is a ready supply of facts.

Reputation

If the new operation is a joint venture, established with the aim of winning new business from other organizations in a similar line of business, the reputation of the new enterprise is paramount. With a mobile workforce, many staff will move between competitors. Workers may perhaps have partners who now work for competitors. There are few industries or sectors where secrets can survive for long.

HELPING STEPHANIE

The fictitious excerpt from Stephanie's diary illustrates a number of phases that an outsourced employee will face during the process. Figure 31.1 tells the same story in graphical form.

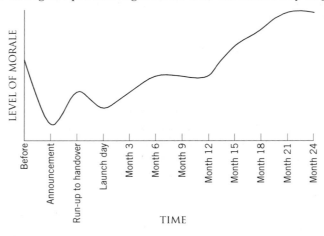

FIGURE 31.1: Stephanie's morale curve

Before the announcement: status quo

This is the point against which subsequent changes can be measured in terms of impact. The level of morale will depend on how staff feel about the nature of work and the work environment. If there have been rumours that the company is going to be outsourced, staff are likely to be hostile and unreceptive. Do not keep employees in the dark, otherwise trust may be irrevocably broken.

Dave Claridge, a principal consultant at KPMG, says:

'The root of the problem lies far earlier in the cycle than most people realize. A typical organization outsourcing a division of the business starts to study the working practices that are currently employed and hold meetings with potential advisors or suppliers. Lots of questions being asked and a regular supply of strangers coming into the office will never go unnoticed. Rumours start, speculation grows – and it is seldom a positive force.'

From here on, the shape of the morale curve is cast. Claridge says that you cannot tell staff too much or too early. He also advises that HR should be engaged right from the start.

Announcement

Staff are likely to be in shock and probably very angry. Make the impact of the announcement as non-traumatic as possible. Communication is key and it should be regular, repeated and consistent. People need to be available to answer questions, otherwise employees will stew and irritation levels will build up.

Run-up to handover

Resentment abounds because staff expect huge changes to their working environment. At this time, staff need a human point of contact. Reassure them about career growth and life after outsourcing. Post everyone an offer letter explaining exactly what their job will be. Tell staff what they should expect to receive as an employee of the new company; stress that they will be taken care of.

Launch day

Usually, there is no great change. Employees are either co-located with the client, or their job is transferred to another office. They realize they are still doing the same job – the only real change is the name above the door. Even if staff have been sufficiently prepared for this, there will still be a feeling of anticlimax.

Claridge believes the answer is to mark the day with real changes:

'Everyone should go home from the office with a clear job description and objectives. They should be given an explanation of the things that matter most to the new business – customer satisfaction, quality and revenue generation. Offer them the opportunity to attend courses to learn more about these things. Finally, plan to establish teams that focus on specific issues. The teams should be cross-functional and work at all levels – for example, a quality improvement task force will need representatives from all parts of the business. All the staff should be told about these teams, their aims, objectives and responsibilities and invited to apply to join them.

At the end of changeover day, everyone will have a clear role, will have seen commitment to change through training programs and will have been given an opportunity to participate actively in the change process.'

Month 3

There should be a general level of acceptance within the outsourced group. Employee skills should be assessed so that the managers in the company know where to look for specific skills. This way, the company will not lose any intellectual capital that could be more widely applied. Employers must find ways to keep employees happy once they make the switch. Suppliers could design innovative work environments that create entirely new job situations for the transitioned employees.

Month 9

Morale will have definitely increased over the last couple of months as staff have settled into new routines and work procedures. Companies should pay particular attention to the role of human resource management at this stage to sustain employee satisfaction.

Month 18

By this stage, the outsourced organization should have taken on new business and staff should be happy. The focus of their jobs should have become the mission of the company they have joined. They are now transitioning from a cost-centre to a revenue-generating mentality. Employees wishing to develop their careers should have opportunities to do so.

EFFECTIVE COMMUNICATION

Clearly, the key is to recognize the stage which each employee is going through, and develop communication strategies to deal with each point in the cycle. For example, there is no point in talking about beneficial changes to terms and conditions at a time when staff are simply concerned for their jobs.

Claridge says:

‹ As soon as there is a strong possibility that outsourcing will occur, I would advise bringing the staff together and telling them as much as you can: "We are considering different ways of delivering our IT services to the business. One option is to bring in organizational change consultants, another is to partner with an outsourcing company, or we could decide to continue to operate as before. Whatever happens, however, these are the ramifications for you . . ." and so on. ›

Once this initial statement has taken place, Claridge advises that key staff are identified and taken aside as early as possible for private conversations.

‹ If the individual sees himself or herself primarily as a technologist, the conversation should emphasize that working for an IT company, the employee will have a much better career path and will be working at the core of the business. But if an employee feels as much a part of the financial services industry as of the technology ecosystem, the conversation should develop more along the lines of: "We would like to talk to you on a separate basis because as we make this transition we are going to need the skills of an individual who can help us understand and deal with the links between the business and the technology." ›

Claridge advises that it is often worthwhile having an agreement in place with the outsourcer to ensure that, whatever staff changes are to be made, nobody will be made compulsorily redundant for the first 12 months. Clearly there is a considerable cost to insisting on such a clause, but it will help to ensure a fast transition with less trauma for all concerned.

Management morale

Curiously, while the morale curve of the employees plummets and then rises slowly, a similar curve for the management team is almost the inverse for the first year or so (Figure 31.2).

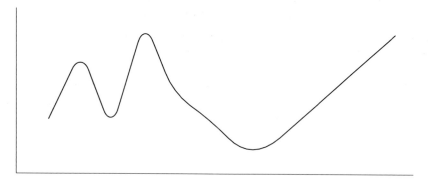

FIGURE 31.2: Management morale curve

When managers are ready to announce the deal, they are excited to have found a radical way to deliver business objectives. Morale falls during negotiations as the full complexity emerges. When the deal is finally signed, there is a huge wave of relief and optimism. But new outsourcing contracts inevitably disappoint in the early stages and key staff may leave, driving down management morale still further. It is often a full year before things settle down and everyone can see the original intended benefits being reaped.

SUMMARY

1   Helping your staff through the transition is not just a moral responsibility – it is vital for the future success of the outsourced operation.

2   Long-term operational staff have unique knowledge of how the organization works. Losing them causes disruption and can lead to inefficiencies, errors and further staff dissatisfaction.

3   Disgruntled ex-staff have the opportunity to do a great deal of harm to your organization.

4   Bear in mind your reputation: workers may have partners or friends who work for competitors (or even customers) ready to capitalize on your internal weaknesses.

5   Counter rumours with a facts. Tell staff as much as possible, as early as possible.

6   After you make the announcement, staff are likely to be shocked and angry. Have people available to answer questions, otherwise employees will stew.

7   In the run-up to handover, continue to offer reassurance. Write staff an offer letter explaining exactly what their job will be. On launch day, there should be evident changes to avoid anticlimax.

8 Find ways to keep staff happy after they have made the switch; for example innovative work environments or new job situations. Bring in human resource management to help sustain employee satisfaction.

9 By the 18-month stage, staff should be happy and focused on the new company's mission. Career development opportunities should be available.

10 Be aware that management morale may take an opposite direction to that of staff. It is often a year or more before things settle down.

PART 4

POLITICS AND THE PUBLIC SECTOR: RED TAPE, GREEN LIGHT

CHAPTER 32

ATTITUDES TO OUTSOURCING WORLDWIDE

This chapter looks at the various attitudes to outsourcing which exist in different countries. The remainder of Part 4 will focus on public sector outsourcing in the UK as a case study, examining the specific issues relating to local government, e-government, schools and the military.

While outsourcing is clearly a business decision, successful implementation of a contract relies heavily on sympathetic legislation being in place. Where government policy is skewed towards labour rights at the cost of business flexibility, outsourcing is difficult to implement profitably.

Other factors are social or cultural. In some countries, loyalty (whether among individuals or between employer and employee) counts more highly than in others. Elsewhere, outsourcing may even still be seen as a sign of desperation by cash-strapped companies, although this view is becoming far less common.

UNITED STATES

In the private sector, US business models tend to be driven by short-term imperatives. Currently, the NYSE demands quarterly reporting of financials from its members – which is causing some resistance now that deregulation is opening them up to wider competition from European and other US markets. According to Phil Morris at Morgan Chambers, outsourcing contracts tend as a result to be very focused on bottom-line savings. Morris notes that the average length of tenure for a CIO/IT director in the US is only 14 months – just long enough for them to join, agree cost objectives, deliver for a year and then pick up the bonus cheque at the end!

In this environment, IT outsourcing will clearly regard saving money above all other considerations. As a consequence, the balance of service quality, people management, strategic advantage and new developments that characterize UK outsourcing contracts is usually markedly less pronounced. Service providers are impelled to put together quick-fix, cost-cutting packages, rather than the more sophisticated deals Europe prefers.

Over the past decade, Congress has moved from being critical of the overuse of private sector contractors to becoming a born-again enthusiast for the potential cost savings, efficiencies and, I suspect, de-politicization of difficult staff-reduction decisions. In a drive to embrace outsourcing in the US Government, the Clinton administration introduced the Federal Activities Reform Act in 1998. This requires all government agencies to provide a list of all the activities they undertake that are 'inherently non-governmental'. The implication was that all such work could be benchmarked against competitive bids from the private sector. A year later, market research firm Input forecast that the new Act would drive a $34 billion opportunity for outsourcing service providers between 1999 and 2004. Clearly this represents a bonanza opportunity for the outsourcing industry, albeit a testing time for US Government employees.

The White House's Office of Management and Budget (OMB) had been tracking outsourcing aggressively for some time, and in 1996 it sponsored a major forum on the issue, along with the General Services Administration. With 500 representatives from the public and private sector present, the OMB outlined a new policy, A-76, which lay down US Government procedures for outsourcing. A-76 is a tool that enables independent benchmarking not just to decide which outsourcer to choose, but to make a rational judgement on the best approach to service delivery – whether in-house, outsourcing, or even acquiring services from another government department. The OMB emphasizes that the process is not designed to promote outsourcing as the optimum or even desired result, but to enable government organizations to choose the best delivery route with certainty.

Traditionally, it has been Republicans who have tended to focus on slimming down government, so it was always likely that the Bush administration would be even more enthusiastic about outsourcing than its predecessor. Sure enough, in 2001, the OMB issued a memorandum directing agencies to compete head-to-head with the private sector for 5 per cent of government jobs, rising to 50 per cent over time. Agencies must now prove they can deliver the inherently non-governmental work competitively.

As you might expect, this new push is initially focusing on IT. As well as the obvious reasons of cost savings and maturity of the supply side, there is another critical factor – demographics. According to an article in *ComputerWorld*,[1] more than 50 per cent of the US Government's 70,000 IT workers are eligible for retirement within the next five years.

EUROPE

Attitudes to outsourcing tend to be strongly led by the actions of governments. The first to wholeheartedly adopt the concept of outsourcing was the UK's Conservative Government of the 1980s. Outsourcing enabled Margaret Thatcher to pursue her belief in small government and free enterprise with relatively little disruption. As the UK's fortunes improved and the country started to climb the European league tables for wealth, productivity (driven in part by North Sea oil revenues) and educational standards, other governments looked on to see what lessons could be learned. Right-wing parties across Europe started to espouse the concepts and benefits of shrinking government infrastructures by bringing in commercial operations (synonymous with efficiency and good management) to take over from public sector groups (seen as backward and inefficient).

From the mid-1980s to the mid-1990s, right-wing parties held power in most major European countries, as the left struggled to redefine its role. Then, in 1997, Tony Blair won a landslide victory in the UK elections for the Labour Party. Many people expected a move back towards

[1] Patrick Thibodean, 'Federal Government Eyes More Outsourcing' in *ComputerWorld*, 18 April 2001.

centralization and the growth of the public sector, but New Labour's 'Third Way' proved surprisingly enthusiastic about private enterprise. The introduction of the Private Finance Initiative (PFI) and Public-Private Partnership (PPP) cemented New Labour's position as an outsourcing-friendly government. Suddenly a 'left-wing' administration was leading the way in innovative outsourcing deals.

Inevitably, parties on the left across Europe watched carefully as Blair took the Labour Party to its strongest position for decades. The Third Way became a popular cry across the continent. Suddenly, the ground rules had changed – no more outsourcing contracts that started when the right was in power and ended when the left took over. Now outsourcing was politically acceptable to both sides, and long-term strategic outsourcing deals became attractive to both governments and suppliers.

According to Morris, the outsourcing industry's thinking has largely followed a pattern that has seen services develop in order of complexity (Figure 32.1).

FIGURE 32.1: Development of the outsourcing industry

Most European countries are a little behind the US and UK in their adoption of, and attitude to, outsourcing in the public sector. Suppliers' thinking is therefore driven, not unreasonably, from these two centres. But coming late to a technology or a management strategy provides the opportunity to play leapfrog. There is no reason, from a client's perspective, why it should not skip FM and IT outsourcing and start with BPO. Morris argues that in many countries, the suppliers are now playing catch-up with the clients.

Today, outsourcing contracts at a government level are common across Europe, yet there are still differences among the various countries.

The UK

After a difficult start to public sector outsourcing (largely caused by inappropriate procurement mechanisms), the UK has redesigned its processes to enable the public to get the best deal. The UK is the only country in Europe which allows an outsourcer to lay people off once it has taken over a government operation, and this extra flexibility has been a strong market driver. By contrast, in other countries outsourcers have found themselves hampered by their inability to cut overcapacity. As a result, when their own businesses are under pressure they are forced to lose staff in projects where resources may already be tight, while keeping on under-used (and possibly under-qualified) people in government contracts.

Deregulation in the UK banking industry has rendered it an extremely enthusiastic adopter of most forms of outsourcing. Today, most UK banks outsource their cash handling, cheque processing and other processes that many would consider core to their business operation.

Interestingly, the UK finance sector is now ahead of most outsourcing service providers in its thinking. The first cheque-processing outsourcing deal was initiated by the Royal Bank of Scotland approaching the market, not by EDS (which ultimately won the deal) or another provider promoting its services. Likewise, the second (iPSL, see Chapter 6) was started by Lloyds TSB.

France and Germany

Late adoption by government has meant that outsourcing has been slower to take off. It is still often perceived as more about cost-cutting than strategic direction. But now that both governments are embracing outsourcing, Morgan Chambers expects a boom in these markets.

One of the challenges for the large multinationals is the complexity of the social benefits system in these countries. Local companies such as Siemens and T-Systems in Germany have done well to capitalize on their knowledge here to gain a strong lead in the market.

Unlike the UK, German banking is very tightly regulated, and this will undoubtedly restrict the breadth of deals that can be struck in this market.

Spain

Robert Morgan, CEO of Morgan Chambers, claims that Spain is still a little further behind in its adoption of outsourcing, but notes that Catalonia is a notable exception. As with other regions, the change has been driven by the enthusiastic adoption of outsourcing by the Catalan government.

Italy

Morris characterizes the Italian market as flexible, yet locally focused. Italian firms tend to do business with Italian companies – preferably those with a strong presence in their city. As a result, most of the outside suppliers looking to break into this market have chosen to do so via minority shareholdings in joint ventures with local companies. Banco Ambrosiano Veneto, for example, chose to outsource to a joint venture between a local firm and T-Systems. Fiat, a true global player with a large proportion of its staff outside Italy, has taken a different route; it has chosen to partner with a non-Italian multinational.

Switzerland

In Switzerland, the law is regionalized by Canton. A contract with a Swiss company may have very different structures in Berne, Geneva and Basle. Switzerland also has the world's tightest privacy controls, and this can have a significant bearing on the way in which services are delivered. When Warburg elected to outsource its IT function to Perot Systems in the 1990s, Guy Warren, now VP of service delivery at Unisys, was on the team.

‘Perot Systems always planned to move the large servers and mainframes into its own data-centre, but under Swiss law it could not physically take the data out of the country because nowhere else could conform to its strict privacy rules. For example, a country where the government can demand access to any data for any reason (e.g. for military, tax or criminal justice purposes) would be out of the question. Perot therefore had to find other ways to achieve its goals for contract profitability.’

The Netherlands

The Netherlands has a very flexible attitude to business and is well respected as a pragmatic European business hub. However, Holland's outsourcing industry has seen peaks and troughs. Morris explains:

‘Outsourcing saw strong adoption in the mid-1990s, but there were a number of high-profile failures. For the past three or four years there have been no major, national deals struck – although this is now beginning to change again.’

Morris puts the problems down to the inexperienced teams that outsourcers rapidly assembled from within the country to meet growing demand. The speed of growth came at the expense of applying global standards and audit processes.

Currently, the Dutch Government is keen on outsourcing, but as in most countries, the pace of change is largely set by the civil service. If the civil service slows things down and a general election takes place before any changes can be initiated, a new government may scrap the project.

Morris forecasts a renewed enthusiasm for outsourcing in The Netherlands over coming years.

THE PACIFIC RIM

Australia and New Zealand have taken an aggressive approach to outsourcing, and indeed the Australian government has undertaken some of the largest outsourcing contracts in the world. For example, in 1998 it signed a US$107 million deal with CSC to deliver IT services across five government departments.

In 1999, the Hong Kong Government, in stark contrast to the expectations of the Chinese-controlled regime, adopted an incredibly enthusiastic tone on outsourcing, proclaiming that two-thirds of all IT projects would be outsourced by 2001.

Even in Japan, where the concepts of loyalty and lifetime employment have been culturally inherent for decades, outsourcing is now becoming more and more familiar. In 1996, Jayne Chace, now VP of marketing and global strategy for the public sector at Unisys, was a project manager for one of the first large outsourcing deals in Japan. A major electronics manufacturer, with a product line that extends from office equipment to heavy engineering, had reviewed its value chain around product development. It concluded that its core competence lay in generating innovative ideas for new processor technologies. In executing those ideas, however, it was taking too long in the development phase, which was slowing its time to market and reducing profitability. It needed an alternative approach – by continuing to take responsibility for the initial ideas, it ensured it kept ownership of the IPR, but by outsourcing the execution to a proven design team, it could be one step ahead of the competition.

At the time, there was a very strong culture of loyalty between employee and employer and a strong expectation of a job for life. Chace recalls:

‘ We had a sales and customer relationship team from Europe, a technical and contracts team from California and a West Coast American corporate culture. Our first hurdle was to manage our way through the huge cultural differences between the US and Japan. The Californian team expected to bring in the legal guys early into the process and – because of the litigious nature of their local market – push for a lot of written commitment, contracts and signatures. However, in Japan, where the central tenet of business transactions is the protection of reputation and honour, this smacked of at best heavy-handedness and at worst distrust of, or even disrespect for, the senior managers’ personal word.

The problem was exacerbated by the fact that the Japanese tend to avoid saying “no” to anybody unless absolutely forced to, as it is considered rude. They have an expectation that giving a minimal level of commitment, dissembling, or simply deferring a decision sends a clear message they are not interested. Unfortunately, enthusiastic commercial teams from the West tend to hear what they want to hear, not the subtle differences between a yes that means yes and a yes that means no. As a result, a lot of “no” decisions were interpreted as potential opportunities. When disappointment inevitably came, it encouraged the commercial guys to push the legal team even further into the foreground. I ensured every client-facing member of the outsourcing team was trained in Japanese business etiquette, in sessions which we held every evening. At those sessions, we would also review progress across the entire program – remember, as well as pulling together American and Japanese cultures, we were also pulling together Europeans with other Europeans, Europeans with Americans, engineers with salesmen and lawyers with everybody else! Next, we repositioned our proposition from an outsourcing contract to a "strategic management alliance". Now the Japanese management team could signal that they were not turning their backs on their employees, a lot of the emotional hurdles were removed.

In the end we delivered the project well ahead of schedule. ʼ

The economic crisis that has engulfed Japan since 1996 has changed attitudes enormously. Jobs for life are no longer expected and outsourcing is now far more common. In the year 2000 alone, IBM Japan signed agreements with Sharp, Nissan and a number of major banks.

SUMMARY

1 Political and cultural factors result in different attitudes to outsourcing in different countries. The US and UK lead the field.

2 The nature of the US market means that outsourcing contracts tend to focus on short-term cost imperatives above other benefits. The current Bush administration's commitment to government outsourcing encourages the market to grow.

3 In Europe, the UK is at the forefront of the industry following enthusiastic backing for outsourcing by successive Conservative and Labour Governments, but newcomers have the ability to 'leapfrog' the traditional FM/IT routes to outsourcing and go straight for full BPO.

4 Although initially slow off the mark, strong outsourcing growth is now expected in France and Germany.

5 Spain is behind other countries in its adoption of outsourcing, with the exception of Catalonia.

6 Italians like doing business with Italians, so many external outsourcers choose to take minority shareholdings in joint ventures with local companies.

7 Switzerland's system of regional government and its stringent privacy laws make outsourcing contracts here extremely complex.

8 The outsourcing market in The Netherlands has experienced peaks and troughs, but future growth is forecast.

9 Australia and New Zealand are aggressive adopters, as is Hong Kong.

10 Inherent cultural attitudes of loyalty and jobs for life slowed the growth of outsourcing in Japan, but since the economic crisis of 1996 the country has become an enthusiastic adopter.

CHAPTER 33

PUBLIC SECTOR OUTSOURCING IN THE UK

ITNet is a UK-focused outsourcing company with its roots in the public sector. Employing around 2500 staff, it offers a broad range of services from ASP to full-blooded, TUPE-based outsourcing.

Originally the IT department of Cadbury Schweppes, ITNet was spun out over a decade ago and has thrived as an outsourcer. Chris Head, a consultant on government IT policy and a lecturer at Henley Management College, sees Cadbury's history as a key reason for ITNet's success in the public sector.

When George Cadbury built his chocolate factory in Bournville, just outside Birmingham, he also built a new town filled with houses that would enable his staff to enjoy a far higher standard of living than was common for factory workers at the time. That sense of paternalism and focus on 'doing right by the workers' continues to pervade the culture at ITNet. This is a key strength for the company in public sector outsourcing deals, especially with local authorities. Councils (especially left-wing councils) are likely to bring workers' represent-atives into the process of selecting an outsourcer, so attitudes to staff will be a critical part of the selection process in many cases.

Paul Johnson, sales director for ITNet's public-sector division, describes the difference between public-sector and private-sector relationships:

> ‘ In the private sector, an engagement can come about very informally – a chat at a party can lead to a meeting in the boardroom that can in turn lead to an informal study and all the way to a major outsourcing implementation. In the public sector, processes are in place to ensure any engagements follow a formalized, accountable procedure. ’

Public sector outsourcing has a poor reputation, even though today it can be very effective. This reputation is driven by two factors. The first is clearly the bad publicity that resulted from a stream of early, high-profile failures; the other is the restricted process.

THE RESTRICTED PROCESS

In order to bring a level of accountability to public sector procurement, a series of processes have been put into place over the past 40 years. This is referred to as the restricted process. In a large-scale procurement, the standard process of provider selection is as follows:

☐ An informal study is undertaken. This can involve as many or as few suppliers as the organization wishes. Concepts and approaches are discussed, but aside from guide-line costs to help with the decision to outsource or not, there are no commercial discussions.

☐ Once the concept has been agreed, and the public sector body has decided to go ahead, the opportunity is then advertised in the *Official Journal of the European Communities* – the standard directory of all government procurement in Europe, more commonly known as the European Journal. The opportunity will usually first be announced as a request for information (RFI), sometimes referred to as a pre-qualification questionnaire (PQQ). Any organization can choose to bid for the business at this stage, although there are likely to be some restrictions over size, trading history, etc. to keep bidders down to a manageable number.

☐ Once the field has been narrowed by evaluating responses against pre-agreed criteria, a formal invitation to tender (ITT) will be sent out to the remaining bidders.

☐ During the process, there is little or no contact allowed between provider and procurer. If a meeting is held with a supplier, it has to be with a pre-agreed agenda and the same meeting must also be offered to every other bidder. Alternatively, all suppliers have to be present. The very high pre-sales costs involved in such tenders means that losing parties may take legal action if they believe there is even the remotest possibility of favouritism. As such, very few public sector bodies risk their position by granting face-to-face meetings before the process is complete and the contract awarded.

☐ There will often be a final shortlist generated and each outsourcer will be invited to bid for 'best and final offer' pricing (BAFO). The public sector body then makes a selection against pre-agreed criteria, but is ultimately driven by price.

☐ Once the selection has been made, due diligence begins and further negotiation will often take place.

☐ Ultimately, the body in question must choose the lowest-cost provider that meets the agreed requirements.

This approach works very well when acquiring capital equipment or looking for a service to deliver a known set of processes in a commonly understood framework. In outsourcing, however, it may not be the best approach. For outsourcing to be successful, there has to be a saving made in terms of either efficiency or economy of scale. Different outsourcers will normally achieve these savings in different ways. Intangible or 'soft' benefits will be calculated in different ways and with different levels of focus. Ultimately, outsourcing contracts that are put together on a win-win basis are too subjective to be realistically measured on the basis of comparing documented approaches and pricing.

With cost as the only point of differentiation of any value, outsourcers are forced to bind tightly the exact nature of the service delivered. Commonly, prices are kept so close to the bone that the provider is forced to rely on 'scope creep' (a requirement for additional chargeable services outside the scope of the original agreement) to ensure it makes a profit.

With margins so tight, there is little room for flexibility, and governance-related reviews can often be uncomfortable as each party looks to fulfil conflicting expectations.

At the same time, such a structured approach involves very high pre-sales costs – ITNet calculates that responding to a Government RFI process can cost between $150,000 and $750,000 depending on the size, duration and number of steps. Remaining engaged in the process is a difficult decision. In a number of cases, government agencies found that most, if not all, of the suppliers chose to pull out before the process was completed.

So what has changed? In 1999, the Government recognized that the restricted process was not delivering results in the best interest of the public. A new, alternative approach was therefore introduced – the negotiated process.

THE NEGOTIATED PROCESS

As with the restricted process, the opportunity to engage with suppliers is tightly controlled, but the process works slightly differently:

☐ Once preliminary discussions have taken place with one or two potential suppliers, the opportunity is advertised in the European Journal as before.

☐ The potential outsourcers are invited to respond to the PQQ or RFI. As before, no contact is allowed until the responses are in and an initial selection has taken place.

☐ The remaining outsourcers are then given an invitation to negotiate (ITN). This is normally restricted to three providers, although it can sometimes be far more.

☐ Due diligence is then entered into, with proposed pricing submitted at this stage.

☐ Negotiation continues until BAFO pricing is submitted.

☐ Unlike the restricted process, once the contract has been awarded there is no scope for further negotiation.

In the main, this is a more successful approach. The negotiated process allows for more candour in the process and gives both parties a far better opportunity to understand the mutual objectives involved. Once the contract is awarded, the governance process can be entered into with a good understanding of the strategies and goals of each party.

SUMMARY

1   In the private sector, outsourcing can happen informally, but the public sector has rigorous, formalized processes in place to which contract bidders must adhere. These, along with high-profile failures, have contributed to its poor reputation.

2   The so-called 'restricted process' for procurement evolved to ensure accountability of third-party suppliers, but its inflexible focus on finding the lowest price, high pre-sales costs for bidders and an inability to negotiate properly makes it unsuitable for most outsourcing contracts.

3   In the late 1990s, the Government introduced the 'negotiated process' which gives both parties more opportunity to understand mutual objectives and put together a successful deal.

CHAPTER 34

LOCAL GOVERNMENT OUTSOURCING

When she became Prime Minister in 1979, an overhaul of local government was high on Margaret Thatcher's list of priorities. Following a stint as Minister for Education, she had worked closely with local authorities, and regarded them as profligate and badly managed. Her answer was to push through the concept of compulsory competitive tendering (CCT). Under new legislation, the local authorities were forced to identify all support services (in US terms, 'inherently non-governmental activities') and put them out to tender. In-house teams were allowed to bid for the business too.

The practical implementation of this legislation proved very difficult. In the face of considerable resistance from the civil service, a reluctance on the part of local authorities themselves and problems with European Union legislation that conflicted with some of the principles of CCT, the process moved very slowly, and largely depended on the political leanings of any given authority.

CCT won through for cleaning, catering and maintenance in most cases, but it was rarely applied to information and communications technology (ICT), human resources or payroll services. In the last months of John Major's Conservative Government (1997), it became apparent to the Labour Party that it was likely to win a landslide majority at the next election, so they initiated a comprehensive consultation process with local authorities as to how they could best engage. Labour was critical of the CCT process, but at the same time recognized that it needed to keep the pressure up to overhaul local authorities' poor track record of service delivery. The result of this process was a new program – Best Value.

BEST VALUE

Best Value replaced CCT and differed in a number of ways:

☐ It focused not on one outsourcing plan, but on continual improvement – even where services have already been outsourced.

☐ It covered all activity, not just support services.

☐ It ran on a rolling four-year cycle.

The Best Value program states that local authorities must evaluate all of their business functions across the entire organization at a rate of 25 per cent per annum. After four years, the entire authority will have been benchmarked and the process begins again with the first 25 per cent. The reviews are based upon a four-step process, commonly referred to as the four Cs:

☐ Challenge.

☐ Consult.

☐ Compare.

☐ Compete.

Challenge

The organization needs to ask itself three questions:

☐ Do we really need to do this?

☐ Could it be done better?

☐ Could it be handled in a different way?

For example, Chris Head, a Best Value specialist and e-learning consultant, recently undertook this process with a local authority evaluating its staff computer education program. IT literacy is a critical step if the authorities are to reach their e-government targets (see Chapter 35).

At the time, the authority was running all of its IT education on the basis of traditional 'chalk 'n' talk'. Courses were run on key applications such as Microsoft Office. There was only a small amount of computer-based training (CBT) in use. Head recommended a shift to focus on CBT as the primary means of delivering skills, backed up by traditional courses – not for full applications, but in short 'just in time' modules, designed to be delivered in two-hour bursts rather than two-day courses. This approach meant that staff spent less time out of the office, the amount of information delivered was more digestible and the content was more relevant.

Consult

The public is canvassed for feedback on services:

☐ Are you getting what you need/want?

☐ Are you getting it quickly enough?

☐ Are you getting it where you need it?

Compare

The organization next needs to ask itself:

☐ How does what we do compare with other local authorities, or other private sector companies?

In order to bring in a level of standardization for this process, SOCITM (The Society of IT Managers, the professional body for senior IT managers in local authorities) has introduced a set of six key performance indicators (KPIs) for benchmarking IT management. All six can be reduced to a single numerical score, ranging from support cost per desktop to a more subjective user satisfaction score.

Interestingly, having run this test for a number of local authorities, SOCITM then applied a similar test to a number of private sector organizations. It concluded that overall the public sector operates at a cost 15–20 per cent *lower* than the private sector. This is largely down to lower salaries and a chronic understaffing problem – many IT operations are running 30 per cent light. The result proved a real surprise for a number of government officials, who were working on the assumption that the private sector had a great deal to teach the local authorities about efficiency.

Once the comparison is completed, the authority must report its findings along with a set of recommendations. Then the government brings in the Audit Commission to validate the findings and make its own recommendations.

Compete

The government, in association with the Audit Commission, declares when an authority must go out to the market for competitive tendering, based on the findings of the previous step. In evaluating the results of the Compare stage, the Audit Commission gives two four-point scores: the first is for quality of service, and the second is for the likelihood of improvement in the near future. Chris Head has analyzed the scores over a large number of authorities, and has found a bell curve distribution for both.

Here, there is a bias towards the poorer side with only a few good councils and none excellent. Clearly, while costs may be competitive, authorities are not delivering to the standard that the government might hope to see.

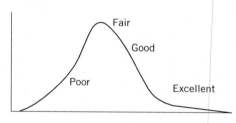

FIGURE 34.1: Quality of service

In Figure 34.2, the bell curve is more evenly distributed, suggesting that either programs for improvement are widely under way, or authorities are adept at managing the Best Value process.

FIGURE 34.2: Likelihood of improvement in the near future

According to Head, the Department of Transportation, Local and Regional Government (DTLR) sees a distribution of IT service delivery quality as in Figure 34.3.

Head believes that the Government is less concerned about the few at the bottom of the scale who will need to undergo radical change, than it is about how to get the bulk of authorities in the middle up to the standard of the upper quartile. Ignoring the obvious mathematical impossibility of having 75 per cent of a data distribution in the upper quartile, the Best Value process – continuous improvement with the threat of enforced outsourcing where in-house teams show no prospect of improvement – should help.

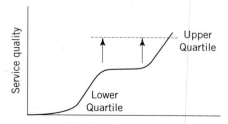

FIGURE 34.3: IT service delivery quality at the DLTR

Benchmarking

Surprisingly, there is no standard procedure for benchmarking. An authority can apply any process it wishes as long as it is rigorous, independent and satisfies the Audit Commission. Some authorities choose to go out to tender as a means of benchmarking, even when they believe their in-house system is unbeatable.

Head is strongly opposed to this approach – tendering is complex and expensive for the outsourcer as well as the authority. Wasting the outsourcers' time with a tender that they cannot win is unethical and pointless. There is also the risk that an outsourcer may put in a loss-leading bid with a view to winning the contract and making back the margins on 'additional charges' later in the process.

Disqualifying a tender can only be done on the basis of terms laid out in the tender document, and the authority could find itself compelled to take on a contract even though both sides know it is likely to be bad business and operates against the original intent of the authority.

Head sees a growth market for an emerging benchmarking industry. Recognized benchmarking companies such as HEDRA are benefiting from this trend, as well as consultants like Head himself.

Best Value and competition

With a lack of standards for benchmarking, the success of the Best Value program to date has been a tribute to the way in which the authorities have worked together through bodies like SOCITM, as well as through a strong sense of cooperation, to pass on best practice ideas and share innovative solutions to universal problems.

There is currently a lot of discussion about applying the league table principle to the Best Value program. Here, authorities would be publicly ranked against one another for progress and service quality. The authorities are concerned that such a step would put up barriers to information sharing and cooperation among them – especially if league table ranking is linked to funding decisions.

SUMMARY

1   In the 1980s, Margaret Thatcher introduced the concept of compulsory competitive tendering (CCT) into local authorities. It was mainly used to outsource distinct support functions. Under Labour, this has evolved into the Best Value program.

2   Best Value covers all activities and focuses on continual improvement. All functions within an authority must be evaluated on a four-year cycle. Reviews are based on a four-step process – the four Cs.

3   Challenge – is the function necessary/being handled in the best way?

4   Consult – the public is canvassed for feedback on services.

5   Compare – how does what you do compare with other authorities/companies? Findings are reported to the government.

6   Compete – the government (with the help of the Audit Commission) declares whether an authority must go out to the market for competitive tendering, based on scores for quality of service and likelihood of improvement.

7   Analysis of authorities' scores shows that few are yet delivering to the expected standard. The Government hopes that the continual improvement process will bring the bulk of average performers up to the standard of the best.

8   There is no benchmarking standard, but it must be rigorous, independent and satisfy the Audit Commission.

9   Do not go out to tender as a means of benchmarking if you have no intention of outsourcing. Wasting providers' time and money with an unwinnable tender is unethical and pointless.

10 The Government is currently considering applying the league table principle to the Best Value program, but authorities are concerned that such a step would put up barriers to cooperation among them.

CHAPTER 35

OUTSOURCING AND E-GOVERNMENT

Since it came to power in 1997, the Blair Government has been pushing local authorities and Whitehall to deliver 'joined-up government'. It is a keen advocate of the use of technology to drive a better service, new levels of efficiency and more choice for the public (in terms of how they interact with government departments and local authorities).

E-government began as a set of airy descriptions of best practice. This caused some concerns for authorities as they tried to keep pace with an agenda that seemed to change with every political speech. Today, however, e-government is now quite comprehensively defined under BVPI 157 – a set of performance indicators that define success. Defining the criteria for such indicators too tightly could render them too unwieldy; at the same time, keeping them too loose leaves them open to abuse.

Currently, the definitions are fairly tight, but there are gaps – for example, there is little reference to time availability. In other words, a local authority can offer a terrific call-centre service for 20 minutes a day and remain fully compliant. Sensibly, the initial approach has been to establish the right spirit of high expectations, but over time the definitions are likely to be enhanced.

FEATURES OF E-GOVERNMENT

The critical elements of e-government are:

☐ Internet-based transactional and information services.

☐ Call-centre services supported by electronic systems rather than heavy administrative processes.

☐ Citizen relationship management systems (also known as customer relationship management or CRM). The best-known of these is Siebel, but smaller, cheaper solutions such as Pivotal and Onyx are gaining ground in the public sector.

☐ Integrated financial and enterprise management systems. Common solutions include SAP and Oracle Financials.

Such systems are often hugely expensive and complex to implement. They also replace existing systems, many of which have been in place for decades and may be running on obsolete technologies. Suddenly there is a deadline for local authorities to do something about their ageing technology infrastructure. This, clearly, represents both a budgetary challenge for authorities and a goldmine opportunity for the outsourcing community (see case study, Chapter 39).

Introducing an outsourcing partner helps in two critical ways:

1　It helps to spread the enormous capital cost over a period of years.

2　It introduces much-needed external skills.

Part of the difficulty for the public sector in embracing such a wholesale change is the lack of mobility within the workforce. It is difficult to see how a London borough can learn from the success of a neighbouring borough, let alone the experiences of another city. Staff employed by a given authority are unlikely to relocate to work for another authority – those who change careers are far more likely to go into the private sector.

In order to address the problem, the Government set up the Pathfinder scheme. Under this, it identified 20 authorities that were felt to be ahead of the e-government curve. They were given government funding towards their activities, in return for a commitment to mentor other authorities going through their own transformations. The Government also engaged marketing consultancy Vantage Point to run a national series of seminars to help promote the message.

In practice, however, while Pathfinder worked well in showing senior staff the principles of e-government, it was perhaps naïve to expect it to explain the practicalities of wholesale system redesign to IT staff. As a result, the majority of local authorities are looking at some form of outsourcing or partnership arrangement to address their e-government requirements.

For local authorities, e-government represents a huge challenge. With public sector outsourcing, it is not just savings that count but any means to spread costs over a longer period of time without affecting the public-sector borrowing requirement (PSBR).

In the UK, local authorities are not allowed to borrow money without express agreement from the Treasury – otherwise it would be impossible for the country to understand its true financial position. Funds for e-government projects must therefore be made available from council budgets, primarily on the IT side.

As the London Borough of Enfield's experiences demonstrate (see case study, Chapter 39), once new systems are in place, there is real scope for return on investment – especially if the new approach means that costly mainframe systems can be switched off and maintenance and service agreements cancelled. But the costs can be huge. When Nike implemented its SAP system, it was reported to have cost the company $500 million. And while a multinational luxury goods provider is a very different scale of operation to a local council, it is clear that the cost of implementing an integrated IT system is far from trivial.

Outsourcing provides scope to use the supplier's cost models: the outsourcer makes the upfront investments and the authority pays for the new systems as a service on an annual basis.

E-GOVERNMENT IN PRACTICE

Tim Dawes, managing director of local government IT consultancy Nineveh Consulting, has been working in the field of local authority IT services for most of his career, both inside and as an external consultant. Dawes is currently working with Braintree, Colchester and Barking and Dagenham, helping them establish their e-government strategies. He says:

‘Implementing e-government is about introducing new ideas and new approaches to long-standing processes. Many local authorities look to some form of commercial partner to provide the conceptual thinking, as well as plugging the skills gaps. The difficulty is choosing a supplier when you cannot articulate what it is you want to buy. After all, if an authority can define what it wants to any reasonable level of granularity, the chances are it does not need an external third-party provider. Much of our time is currently spent helping authorities through this paradox.’

Nineveh normally recommends that the selection process should start using the restricted process to develop a shortlist of potential partnership candidates. The restricted process leaves relatively little scope for outsourcers to demonstrate innovative thinking, but it keeps things simpler, cuts administrative costs and makes the cost of responding much lower for the providers. Once the shortlist has been established, a negotiated process can begin. Having fewer suppliers in the process at this stage means that it is less costly and more manageable for the authority. In addition, the suppliers have a greater chance of offsetting the high cost of the tendering process.

Dawes lays out four steps for e-government partner selection:

1   Prepare a list of potential suppliers. The European Union recommends five, but Dawes sees this as too many:

    ‘Tendering for e-government projects is expensive and time-consuming for outsourcers. If there are too many involved they will be discouraged from entering into the process or, worse still, field the B-team. At the same time, reviewing a response is an expensive and resource-intensive process, so the fewer the better.’

    One approach recommended by consultant Chris Head for keeping outsourcers on side is to ensure they stand to gain from the process, win or lose. For example, it may be possible to agree that all bidders get to see the responses and feedback for every competitor. That way, even if they lose, all concerned will have gained competitive insight and market knowledge to better equip them to win next time.

2   On the same basis, look to reduce the number of candidates under consideration as early as you can in the process. Again, this cuts workload and motivates the suppliers. How do you select at this early stage? Dawes says:

    ‘You will have a good idea of their skills and culture. If you are going to work in partnership, these are the two most important factors – they may have technically brilliant teams, but if they do not work well alongside your in-house staff, or map onto your own cultural and political aspirations, the project will not fly.’

3   Allow each bidder two weeks of access to your entire organization, from the chief executive/council leader downwards. Dawes says:

    ‘The more informed the supplier, the better the quality of the final proposal, the fewer the nasty surprises after the contract has been awarded and the more motivated it will be to stick with the project – after all, access to senior staff is the strongest sign that you are serious and committed to both the outsourcer and the project,’

149

4 Benchmarking costs is very difficult when you are buying innovative strategic input, but there are always elements that can be split out. Dawes says:

‹ Identify isolated slices of the project that can be clearly defined and look for indicative pricing. It can also be worthwhile asking for indicative day-rate pricing. The government procurement agreement (G-CATII) includes a subset called S-CAT which lays out definitions and day rates for different, specifically defined levels of expertise – as well as providing an instant way to compare prices. Remember though that S-CAT only provides time-and-materials-based costs. ›

BRAINTREE DISTRICT COUNCIL

At Braintree District Council, Nineveh helped build an innovative solution to the challenge of writing a $4.5 million, three-year contract to deliver a fundamentally unknown service. Braintree identified that there could be up to 20 projects over three years which would move it towards fully joined-up e-government. At the same time, it had to be certain that each project stood up as a viable investment in its own right. This section is based on an interview with Tim Dawes, Managing Director of Nineveh Consulting Ltd.

The contract was arranged such that the outsourcer would work with the council to prepare a business case for each project. Referred to as a project assessment process (PAP), the document would include a project plan and a return on investment (ROI) analysis. Once the project was given the go-ahead, the supplier would be paid 25 per cent of the total agreed cost of the project. Once the project was completed, the supplier would then see the next 25 per cent (completion is defined as the time user acceptance testing is signed off).

Unusually, the remaining 50 per cent would only be paid when the business benefits laid out in the original PAP had been achieved. This would reduce the council's exposure to failed projects and keep the business cases firmly rooted in reality. The PAP had to be negotiated between the outsourcer and the council to ensure both sides were comfortable with their commitments. Agreeing on the PAP was every bit as important as agreeing on the rest of the contract, service levels and governance processes.

Clearly, demonstrating new service delivery or a reduction in processing time on a tightly defined transaction is relatively straightforward, but some benefits are harder to quantify – for example, improvements to the quality of management information. Here, internal customer satisfaction surveys or very specific report definitions may be needed.

The Braintree model can lead to the following scenarios:

☐ The best case – all 20 PAP documents are signed off and the projects delivered successfully. In this case, the outsourcer sees maximum revenues and the council makes maximum headway towards its objectives. Everybody wins.

☐ None of the projects are signed off. Here both sides lose out – the council on progress, the outsourcer on revenue – but at least the costs are contained.

☐ A proportion of the projects are approved and delivered successfully – a clear win-win situation.

☐ A number of projects receive the go-ahead, but do not meet objectives. Here the risk is split – the council has paid 50 per cent of the cost of the projects and not seen the return it expected, while the outsourcer has only seen 50 per cent of payment for the work it has undertaken. Both sides lose, but the exposure is shared. Assuming that the council has seen some of the expected benefits and the outsourcer has recovered most of its costs in the initial 50 per cent, the exposure is small on both sides.

Governance at Braintree

The Braintree agreement also included delivery of basic IT services measured against an SLA as you would expect. Alongside the basic contract, however, there is also a joint statement of working approaches (written as a schedule to the main contract). It is this, rather than the SLA, that governs the approach to the e-government projects. The SLA does not apply to the PAP projects. Instead, the key performance indicators are established up front for every project in the PAP document.

Braintree and ITNet have established a joint executive board. The group has four representatives from the council (the leader of the council, the finance director, the e-government officer and a senior project director). It also has a similar number of executive-level members from ITNet. It is tasked with giving the go-ahead to projects based upon the business cases in the PAP submissions. Crucially, for a project to get the green light, it has to be approved by a majority of both the council and ITNet. With an annual discretionary budget of $1.5 million, the effective and cooperative working of this board is key to the partnership's success.

SUMMARY

1   The Blair Government has been a keen advocate of e-government – using new information and communication technologies to improve local authority and central government services.

2   The critical elements of e-government are: internet-based services, electronic call-centre services, CRM and integrated financial and enterprise management systems.

3   Outsourcing helps spread the enormous capital cost of such systems and introduces much-needed external skills. It is the chosen route for most authorities.

4   Keep selection costs down by using the restricted process to develop an initial shortlist of potential partnership candidates. You can then move to a negotiated process for the remaining bidders.

5   Keep the number of bidders to a minimum. Tendering for e-government projects is expensive for both sides – the fewer bidders, the cheaper the process.

6   Shortlist on the basis of suppliers' skills and cultural fit with your organization. Show that you are committed by allowing each shortlisted bidder two weeks' access to your entire organization, including senior staff.

7   Benchmarking costs is difficult, but certain elements such as time and materials can be split out and costed according to set government definitions as an instant means to compare prices.

8   The example of Braintree District Council shows how outsourcers and authorities can work together and develop innovative solutions to challenges using appropriate risk/reward models and governance structures.

CHAPTER 36

MILITARY OUTSOURCING

❛Mercenaries are disunited, thirsty for power, undisciplined and disloyal; they are brave among their friends and cowards before the enemy . . . The reason for all this is that there is no loyalty or inducement to keep them on the field apart from the little they are paid, and this is not enough to make them want to die for you.❜ – Niccolo Machiavelli, *The Prince, 1514*[1]

AN ETHICAL DILEMMA

In recent years, there has been an increasing rumble on more radical websites about military outsourcing (private military companies or PMCs), particularly (but not exclusively) around US actions in Colombia. Finding unemotional data among the shock-horror reporting is difficult, but there are a number of large PMCs, including Military Professional Resources Incorporated (MPRI), Sandline (which came to UK prominence in a dispute with the British Government over operations in Sierra Leone in the late 1990s) and Dyncorp, which is providing military personnel, law enforcement and third-party training services.

In a report for the website CorpWatch,[2] Jeremy Bigwood reviewed the actions of an armed 'airmobile' search and rescue operation. Unusually, the team in question did not consist of US Army personnel, but staff of Dyncorp. Bigwood likens this new approach to 'the old English "privateer" pirates of the Caribbean 500 years ago, sailing under no national flag – robbing and plundering Latin America's riches for the English Crown'.

Many human rights organizations are now watching these companies, which they perceive as secretive and shadowy. (In their defence, suppliers of covert operational skills can hardly be anything else.) The organizations themselves argue that they have a critical role to play. Sandline is particularly outspoken. Its stated position is:

❛Our purpose is to offer governments and other legitimate organizations specialist military expertise at a time when western national desire to provide active support to friendly governments, and to support them in conflict resolution, has materially decreased, as has their capability to do so.❜

[1] Niccolo Machiavelli, *The Prince* (translated by George Bull) Penguin Books, 2000.
[2] Jeremy Bigwood, 'DynCorp in Colombia: Outsourcing the Drug War' in CorpWatch report, 23 May 2000, www.corpwatch.org.

Sandline takes a strong moral position, stating that it will not work with terrorist organizations (although this has always been a subjective term), drug cartels, embargoed regimes or 'any activity which breaches the basic law of armed conflict'. But whereas most such organizations tend to stay out of the public eye, Sandline has been a consistent defender of the PMC principle. With a portfolio of services that includes PR alongside surveillance, psychological operations and law enforcement, it is perhaps less of a surprise that it is taking on the role of defender of its own business model.

For example, the Sandline website links to a challenging and pretty well-informed article by David Shearer which argues the moral rectitude of using private military services to support the United Nations.[3]

Shearer describes the UN's problems in securing resources to support enforcement in countries that are of limited strategic value to the West. As an example, the article points out that in May 2001, 88 states had pledged a total of 147,900 troops to support the UN, yet the specific request for support in the Congo and Sierra Leone released very few resources. Shearer argues that only poor countries provide resources for such conflicts, because they need the payments the UN makes, whereas the richest and best equipped nations find the financial incentive unattractive and the political downside of heavy casualties far from home a powerful disincentive.

In short, soldiers in poor nations are more likely to be casualties. Shearer concludes:

❛ As a result, militaries of woeful quality are pushed forward. For many poorer states, the prospect of earning around $1 million a month for each battalion contributed to a UN peacekeeping mission is the chief incentive. Quality then becomes the casualty. A soldier's rifle from one of the United Nations Mission in Sierra Leone's (UNAMSIL's) African contingents manning a strategic forward bunker, for example, was found to have only two bullets in it when checked. His battalion's mortars had not been test-fired and most of its other equipment was broken. "We would have liked to have seen some of the governments with capacity, with good armies and well-trained soldiers, participate," said [Kofi] Annan [General Secretary of the United Nations], "but they are not running forward to contribute to this force." ❜

Shearer's argument is clear – if the UN is to rely on soldiers who are serving in return for payment to their masters, why not take the next logical stage and go to a force for which the money would have more significance and which is fully trained, properly equipped and not subject to changes of strategy driven by domestic politics?

Which side is right? To a large degree, the challenge lies not in the principle of military outsourcing but in the governance processes. Legal and congressional systems of accountability have developed over hundreds of years on the assumption that military action is undertaken by the military. According to Bigwood's CorpWatch article, with outsourced military action only a select few in Congress need know of their activities, and their operations are not subject to public scrutiny despite the fact they are on the government payroll.

Having never been a great subscriber to conspiracy theories, I am inclined to believe that outsourced military services are more a function of cost savings and the need to inject specialist skills than anything underhanded, but politically this is clearly a sensitive issue. It must also be a temptation for governments to shield the public from news about 'our boys dying on foreign soil' when the conflict is far from home and where it is difficult for the electorate to see how the specific military threat translates to a risk to their own way of life.

[3] David Shearer, 'Privatising Protection' in *World Today*, August/September 2001, www.riia.org/wt.html.

Bigwood points out that military outsourcing is not new, but its scale is changing dramatically:

‛Outsourcing belligerent activities on the part of the US Government is not new. It goes back to the Revolutionary War. Many such companies were involved in the Vietnam war, but they were only a minuscule presence compared to the major military effort by the US there. What is new is that now contract employees are in the forefront of operations. In the Colombian war, private outsourced military men are out on the frontlines, while the real US troops are hidden on bases as trainers’.

Writing in the *St Petersburg Times* in December 2000,[4] Paul De La Garza and David Adams cite a substantial, $6 million deal with MPRI to provide ground-based services, also in Colombia. The article raises similar issues and concerns about accountability as the CorpWatch piece.

As the radical press continues to raise the issue, the law may change – one US Senator, Janice Schakowsky, has now submitted the Andean Region Contractor Accountability Act, 'legislation that would prohibit US funds from being used to contract with private military companies in the Andean region'.

Arguing that the outsourcing of military services is a threat to transparancy and accountability, Schakowsky is currently working to drive through the legislation. Whether she is successful or not, one cannot help feeling that the issue is not so much about who does what, as who knows what, and who is ultimately accountable for any actions.

SUMMARY

1   Military outsourcing – the use of private military companies (PMCs) by governments and international organizations such as the UN – is a highly sensitive issue politically and is subject to scrutiny from a raft of campaigning organizations.

2   Campaigners argue that PMCs are shadowy and unaccountable.

3   Military outsourcers such as Sandline counter that they only work with non-embargoed governments and legitimate organizations that have a genuine need for their military expertise.

4   They point to arguments which show that PMCs are more suitable for use in conflicts where national governments have little vested interest and therefore no desire to risk casualties among their own citizens.

5   Despite such claims, the key reason for using PMCs is probably cost savings.

6   Public accountability is a genuine concern, and there are legislative moves under way in the US to increase transparency.

4 Paul De La Garza and David Adams, 'Military Aid . . . From The Private Sector' in *St Petersburg Times*, 3 December 2000.

CHAPTER 37

CONCLUSION

PUBLIC SECTOR OUTSOURCING – A POLITICAL TIME BOMB?

In many outsourcing projects, the primary motivation for the public sector body is to achieve upfront investment in new systems. Suppliers will always be willing to work on this basis, as long as the appropriate safeguards are in place and the contract is sufficiently long to allow them to recover their investment, cover the cost of money, fund their risk and leave them with a reasonable profit. A typical public sector outsourcing contract is set for ten years. As the contract matures, the outsourcer's margins will grow, with break-even point around the end of the third year.

But fast-forward five years. The investments in new technology made by the outsourcer are now looking a little out of date. The authority has paid for the outsourcer's investments and the margins for these groups are now very strong. The Sunday newspapers start to highlight the substantial profits which contractors are making from these relationships, and the fact that they still have many years left to run, probably at ever-growing margin levels. The upfront investments, risks and heavy skills injection that occurred five years ago are largely forgotten in the rush for headlines. There is mounting political pressure to break (or at least renegotiate) some of these contracts.

How can this issue be avoided? It is essential that this scenario is predicted, understood and addressed at the beginning of the contract. The outsourcer needs to be in a position to demonstrate ongoing value and to rationalize the margin structure to a sceptical audience.

In the meantime, those contracts that stay within the original projected costs should be budgeted in advance and remain under the radar. It is those contracts where the outsourcer is fighting to increase scope (and therefore introduce new charges) where negative publicity is more likely to arise.

By building contracts that enable the outsourcer to make a fair margin without resorting to these measures, the risk will be cut. Constructing careful contracts to limit the outsourcer's ability to take this approach will help. For example, consultant Chris Head advises that authorities should have a clause which states:

'The outsourcer will have as clear a view of future legislative changes that may affect the scope of the contract as the authority does. It will therefore carry the risk that changes to legislation may drive a requirement to expand or change the scope of the initial project. '

Part 5 will explore the future of outsourcing in more detail. Part 4 ends with a case study of the London Borough of Enfield's approach to IT outsourcing.

CHAPTER 38

CASE STUDY: LONDON BOROUGH OF ENFIELD

In 1999, the London Borough of Enfield went out to tender for a partnership-based IT outsourcing solution. It used the negotiated process to identify a partner that could work 'with us rather than for us' and deliver the new functionality needed while generating cost savings. It selected ITNet, the Birmingham-based outsourcer that specializes in local government solutions. This case study evaluates the strategy involved, but also the financials – critical given that cost is the primary driver for all outsourcing activity. This section is based on an interview with Paul Johnson, ITNet's Director of Sales and Marketing.

THE PROBLEM

As government initiatives around e-government began to emerge in early 1999, it became apparent that Enfield's largely monolithic, mainframe-based accounting systems were going to cause a problem. At the same time, the systems were hampering the council's efforts to introduce a more devolved management structure. It needed specialists simply to interpret the reports coming from the systems, which was slowing down decisions and adding cost.

The council had to replace its old mainframe equipment and software with a financial system that would meet the new structural needs, but that would also put the council in a position to meet e-government targets. It had identified SAP as the most appropriate software to achieve its aims.

The challenge

Unfortunately, budgetary constraints prevented the council from taking the traditional route of procuring new technology, so it decided that outsourcing offered the best way forward.

ITNet took a strategic approach, building the system using a standard template that it ensured would be equally applicable to other local authorities. It then chose to deliver the application from its own remote data-centres (an ASP model). This enabled ITNet to keep costs down, minimize disruption, but also to create an asset that could be sold to further

157

local authorities, and therefore provide competitive advantage and a potential new revenue stream.

THE RESULTS

☐ The council can now feed up-to-date financial data to the newly devolved business managers across its 10,000 staff. With better information, better decisions can be made and accountability becomes more transparent.

☐ The reports are easy to understand, so specialist interpreters are no longer required.

☐ The new, hosted system has allowed Enfield to remove the need for the mainframe, which will drive substantial savings on maintenance costs and lease payments.

☐ The new systems put the council in a strong position as the Government's modernizing agenda continues to unfold. For example, the system can be readily integrated into a CRM solution when required. Ultimately, councils will have to be able to communicate with citizens in person, electronically or by telephone, with equally strong levels of service provided whichever channel is employed. CRM and multi-channel packages will play a major part in these initiatives, and the new SAP-based financial system is ready to connect to all of the major suppliers' products when required.

The Financials

According to Paul Johnson, director of sales and marketing at ITNet, the figures worked out as follows. The contract runs for ten years. Prior to the outsourcing agreement, the council was spending $12 million a year on IT.

A large part of the cost was the lease payment and maintenance of the ICL mainframe system. This had 18 months to run (assuming that the council could migrate its systems off the machine during that time). Post-outsourcing, the council's cost fell by $1.5 million per annum. ITNet received the lion's share of the newly reduced budget, with the balance going to other suppliers.

ITNet contracted to provide a rolling, three-year technology refresh on all desktop equipment so that the council could be confident of staying up to date over the life of the contract. It spent an estimated $16–18 million in the first year of the contract. A large part of this went on development of the new SAP solution. ITNet made this investment partly on the basis that the solution would be repeatable and could generate incremental revenue in other councils.

All equipment was provided on an open-book basis. In other words, the council can audit the cost prices of all equipment being purchased and ITNet is limited as to the percentage mark-up it can add.

ITNet will be in a position to switch off the ICL mainframe when the lease ends, generating a substantial annual saving that will help offset the initial investment.

PART 5

THE FUTURE OF OUTSOURCING: VIRTUAL VISIONS

CHAPTER 39

BANDWIDTH AND BIG SYSTEMS

The extraordinary boom and bust of the telecoms industry over the past five years has left the world with a vast oversupply of bandwidth (network capacity) for sending data around the globe. Companies like Global Crossing, WorldComm, Qwest and NTL built vast networks (fuelled by huge stock valuations), before bursting, South-Sea-Bubble-like, when the investment community suddenly woke up, nursing their collective technology, media and telecommunications (TMT) hangovers.

In the meantime, the big established players had no choice but to update and expand their own networks to protect their market positions. BT, Cable & Wireless and all their global competitors piled into the winner-takes-all bandwidth race.

The result? Today only around 15 per cent of the world's networking capacity is in use.

With a vast supply of connectivity around the globe, commodity pricing to access it, and each owner trying to generate something rather than nothing from the capacity, hardware suppliers' traditional supply chains are starting to look outdated (Figure 39.1).

FIGURE 39.1: Traditional supply chain of a hardware supplier

Large systems are typically built in expensive, G7 countries close to the engineering centres that designed them. They are then assembled into fully working configurations and thoroughly tested before they leave the factory. Once tested successfully, the systems are then disassembled again for safe transportation. They are then freighted to appropriate distribution hubs.

This is an expensive process as the systems are:

- ☐ Heavy.
- ☐ Fragile.
- ☐ Temperature sensitive.
- ☐ Usually shipped in batches of containers.

Once at the hub, the systems are then reassembled and often software is loaded. They are then shipped on again, usually by road, either to a third party that will often repeat the whole process yet again, or direct to the customer site where they are commissioned, installed and tested for the third or fourth time.

Ridiculous, isn't it? In a world with virtually unlimited bandwidth, why not build the systems in a low-cost environment outside the G7 community, and then ship them next door to a mega data-centre where the customers can connect directly over secure communication lines? Costs are very much lower, opportunities for errors fall by an order of magnitude, customers' relationships with the supplier are improved. This shift therefore seems inevitable.

But it is not just the margins that will improve for the hardware suppliers – bringing all the technology into a single, secure location also gives them competitive advantage over the pure IT outsourcing players such as EDS or CSC.

CHAPTER 40

THE DEATH OF IN-HOUSE IT

According to the Morgan Chambers/*CW360* survey,[1] around half of all IT staff now work for an outsourcer. Although trend analysis is always dangerous, it seems likely that by 2010 there will be very few large, home-grown IT departments left.

Already, with outsourcers providing the strongest CV assets and the best environment for an IT professional who wants to be at the centre rather than the periphery of the business, it is likely that an ambitious graduate who wants to make a career in computing will have the big outsourcers at the top of his or her list of ideal employers. As in-house IT becomes the minority approach, new staff are less likely to consider approaching large companies directly, naturally assuming that the right route into the job is through EDS, CSC or IBM.

To attract employees, the in-house teams will therefore have to become more pro-active, or bring staff across from non-technical roles and cross-train. Given the limitations these groups are likely to have with salary budgets and the authority to invest capital budget in recruitment programs, I predict that the recruitment process will get harder and harder.

Organizations with a heavy dependence on proprietary mainframe technology already face an impending skills crisis. Most mainframe technicians are aged over 50 years; new graduates are simply not turned on by Cobol, batch runs or CICS – they want to get their hands dirty with technologies that are quick to develop, look good and offer the prospects of a lucrative contractor lifestyle should the job market become too difficult at any time. Microsoft, Java, Sun and Oracle all attract IT staff who have the luxury of choice. As such, many large corporations are in a situation where their critical systems are now only understood by a handful of key staff, all of whom are due to retire within the next five to ten years.

These organizations have a stark choice – migrate, or keep paying whatever this tiny remaining skills pool demands. Migration sounds attractive, but most major corporations around the world have tried and failed migration programs from mainframes. While the economics may stack up in theory, the practicalities show that migrating a system from one platform to another is a recipe for disaster.

163

[1] Morgan Chambers and *CW360*, *Outsourcing in the FTSE 100 – The Definitive Study*, 2001.

☐ If it goes perfectly, the new system will do exactly the same as the old one.

☐ If anything goes wrong, the new system will be worse than the old system it replaces – you can therefore lose, but not win.

☐ The old systems have typically been running successfully for decades. They are often cumbersome and inflexible, but almost invariably stable.

☐ New systems crash more than old systems.

☐ Building new systems from lower-cost, more open technologies is not difficult, but matching mainframe levels of reliability and availability is very difficult – and very expensive.

☐ Obtaining capital budget for rewriting a system that will be functionally the same as the old one is (at best) extremely difficult.

For these companies, outsourcing may well be the only route available. Outsourcers may not be overrun with mainframe experts, but they will at least have a concentration of skills that can be applied in a variety of organizations, and the financial models to allow them to invest in mainframe conversion early in a contract, in return for operational cost savings over the longer term (see London Borough of Enfield case study, Chapter 38).

CHAPTER 41

TECHNOLOGY COMMODITIZATION

If IT is being delivered as a service to the majority of organizations, large and small, the question of brand value and technology preferences will cease to touch these organizations directly. The *how* of the delivery process will be the responsibility of the outsourcers, while the clients will (in theory at least) be concerned only with the *what*.

An outsourcer will make technology decisions on a very different basis to a client. Issues such as technology, service packages and brand value will count for little. For the outsourcer, the priorities will be:

- ☐ Non-competitive positioning.
- ☐ Commercial terms.
- ☐ Willingness to share risk.
- ☐ Non-functional requirements (scalability, availability, manageability).
- ☐ Logistics.
- ☐ Flexibility, both commercial and technological.
- ☐ Credit terms.

For the mainframe suppliers, the future probably lies with them selling their own technology as a service (as seen in Chapter 39). This will prove an interesting competitive challenge to the existing outsourcers. For the other technology suppliers, all bets are off.

The smart outsourcer will be building solutions that meet customers' objectives on the most efficient basis, but will also be focused on keeping its options open. This translates into building IT strategies that avoid supplier lock-in at all levels. Technology suppliers themselves are fighting to offer independence from all the other technologies in return for a commitment to their own, and this is a minefield to navigate:

- ☐ Application server vendors such as BEA offer 'platform independence' for developers. Write your systems using BEA's Weblogic and you can change your mind about the database, the operating system or the underlying hardware at any time in the future. But you have to stick with Weblogic.

☐ Microsoft makes up for its lack of openness with ubiquity. Every other technology vendor has to work with Microsoft if it is to gain access to the majority of the market. This may sound cynical, but it makes sense. The IT industry has an appalling track record of building and adhering to standards. As one commentator put it: 'I love IT standards – there are always so many to choose from.' Microsoft's clout also ensures there are always plenty of skills available, wherever their strategy leads. In the Microsoft world, there is no need for expensive, proprietary (sometimes called 'open') hardware. In short, with Microsoft you are free to choose the lowest-cost hardware and from a vast array of application packages and tools.

☐ Oracle has built a database-centric view of the world. If you build your application using Oracle, you can run it on virtually any operating system you like (even Microsoft's) and on nearly every hardware platform, either proprietary or commodity.

☐ Intel offers the greatest amount of processing power for the lowest cost and supports a variety of operating systems, but primarily Microsoft Windows or Linux/Unix. With Intel, costs are very low and flexibility is very high. Even if you cannot quite do it with the technology right now, Moore's Law (the power of computer processors doubles every two years) suggests that you will be able to in a couple of months' time. With Intel, you have complete freedom of choice over which of the people who put its processors into PCs and servers you wish to trade with.

Outsourcers have to develop strategies to give themselves the maximum bargaining strength with each of these suppliers to ensure they can maximize margins and drive the best deal for clients. They then have to balance these in-house strategies with the execution of those strategies in given customer situations where there are technology preferences, skills bases and specific technology drivers.

Right at the bottom of the pile, however, are the hardware suppliers. With all the above options, outsourcers can build every system with anti-lock-in measures at every stage. You do not like Sun's pricing strategy? No problem – migrate the Oracle system over to Linux or even Windows. Unhappy about the rate of growth of the Intel server farm? Switch to a Unisys ES7000 and consolidate onto a couple of huge Wintel machines, or ditch the lot and recompile the Weblogic system to run on an HP Superdome. HP just increased its maintenance prices on the UX servers? Go back to the Linux source code for the HPUX system and recompile it for the IBM X-series machines running AIX . . . and so on.

But if the server suppliers have a headache, the PC manufacturers have full-blown migraines. Already commoditized, the market beyond the home user in an outsourced world will inevitably be dominated by a handful of outsourcer mega-deals, renegotiated regularly in an environment where the outsourcers hold all the cards.

CHAPTER 42

ASP AGGREGATION

While a handful of ASPs have tried to offer a complete managed IT service for full suites of applications (see Chapter 15), there is some doubt about the scalability of this model. If the volume of different supported applications grows beyond a certain number per connected user, it is difficult to see how economies of scale can be maintained. The most likely result is that as these companies grow, they will start to restrict the number of applications that they are willing to support.

For the client, that leaves three unpalatable choices:

1 Migrate off the more obscure applications.

2 Choose to support the non-covered applications in-house.

3 Find another service provider to handle that application, and have the first one support all the others.

On the face of it, none of these options sounds particularly attractive. Migration means hassle, retraining and demonstrable inflexibility for the users – all of which completely defeats the object of outsourcing in the first place. Outsourcing all the applications bar one is equally self-defeating. You still have to retain in-house IT skills for the odd application, thus you are now paying for the ASP's infrastructure as well as your own. Your costs will almost certainly be higher than they were before you started, and getting the ASP to take responsibility for the quality of service will be problematic because it does not own the entire environment. Option three is no better – two, three or more service providers to manage, connect to, apportion blame among, pay monthly fees to, etc.

There is, however, an alternative approach built around the third option – the ASP aggregator. The aggregator builds a portfolio of ASP partners, each delivering an element of the application set. It takes responsibility for service quality, integration and blame-management and provides a single connection point. It has a strong business model, taking a margin on services delivered through other people's expensive infrastructures.

This, however, is an idea whose time has yet to come. There are not yet enough ASPs out there to aggregate – and most of them are in such a parlous financial state that undertaking responsibility for continuation of service for the clients sounds distinctly unappealing.

CHAPTER 43

THE FM
SHOWDOWN

Pest control, road mending, air-conditioning parts and security. Can you imagine four industries with less in common?

Rentokil Initial, Amey Construction, Johnson Controls and Securicor are all long-established businesses with track records in these areas (The Prufrock Column, *The Sunday Times* refers to Sir Clive Thompson, CEO of Rentokil Initial, as 'rat-catcher-in-chief'). Yet, read these companies' documentation and it is clear that they all see themselves heading for the same market:

☐ Rentokil Initial Management Services says that it provides 'a flexible management solution for organizations that seek to outsource a wider range of their non-core management and support service requirements'.

☐ Amey claims to 'provide the broadest range of support services in its sector to public and private organizations, as well as being an owner of large-scale transportation infrastructure concessions'. Its information services division provides 'outsourced information and technology services to clients whose requirements are challenging and demanding, in environments that are dynamic, complex and at times in need of maximum security'.

☐ Johnson Controls regards itself as a 'leading worldwide supplier of building control systems, services and integrated facility management to education, health care, office, government, retail and telecommunication sectors'.

☐ Securicor states that it is 'an international business-to-business group specializing in security, distribution and communication services'. The mission of its information systems division 'is to demonstrate excellence to our customers as a leading integrator of communications, information technology, mobile information technology and mobile asset management, providing life-cycle support through managed support services'.

As the free market continues to impel suppliers to become ever more competitive, they are forced to look for value-added service opportunities – ways to move from being commodity suppliers to strategic service providers, in order to increase margin opportunities.

To make that shift, they know that they have to penetrate the boardroom. A relationship doomed to languish forever in the hands of a procurement officer is never likely to generate margin growth. A packed board meeting agenda is unlikely to squeeze in much time for a frank discussion about pest control or the future of the staff canteen.

These non-core service providers have all recognized that they need to be able to present a total service offer to the executive of their target customers: 'Come with us and we will handle the day-to-day operation of every aspect of your business which is non-core and therefore distracts you from your primary focus.'

Where does this end? In long-standing FM sectors like contract cleaning and security, a balance has been struck, with a handful of large players dominating each sector. As the suppliers move up a level, expect another round of fierce consolidation as the major players strive to expand their service portfolio to deliver a complete solution while locking out new competitors. Rentokil Initial, Johnson Controls, Amey and Securicor may not be direct competitors yet . . . but they soon will be.

CHAPTER 44

THOUGHT LEADERSHIP AND INNOVATION

This book has reported a number of exceptionally bold new initiatives:

☐ The Royal Bank of Scotland outsourcing its cheque processing to EDS.

☐ Lloyds TSB taking this idea much further and building a whole new business venture involving Barclays, Unisys and, later, HSBC to handle the same process.

☐ JP Morgan driving its suppliers to build a new kind of coalition for service delivery – the Pinnacle Alliance.

☐ The British Government developing the Private Finance Initiative (PFI), later refined into the Public-Private Partnership (PPP) program, arguably the most sophositicated of BPO models.

Apart from the obvious connection that each is innovative in their own way, what links all of these initiatives is that they were conceived and driven through not by the suppliers but by the clients.

As all of the functionally managed service providers scrabble to climb the value chain by delivering more complete BPO solutions, it is inevitable that the BPO market will become more crowded (see Chapter 13). As with any other market, as more suppliers enter the fray, supply outstrips demand, margins fall and services start to commoditize. Ultimately, the race will not be won by the swiftest, but by the most imaginative. Service vendors need to develop strategies to keep their thinking ahead of their clients – if the client is driving the ideas, it will inevitably regard all the suppliers as similar. Selection will be based upon whether outsourcers can meet the specification and at what cost.

Outsourcers must find a way to take a strategic leadership role, not just at the bid stage, but before the engagement begins, during the contractual process and constantly thereafter.

Imaginative thinking is a constant challenge for vendors. According to Robert Morgan of Morgan Chambers, a lack of innovative thinking is the single biggest cause of disappointment in the outsourcing market:

Clients are often sold on the fact that bringing in a new, state-of-the-art skills pool will drive innovation. In practice they find they get operational improvements that amount to doing the same stuff as before but better, as distinct from doing better stuff.

Outsourcers are quick to protest. Paul Johnson from ITNet says:

The problem we face, particularly with government, is that when we do put forward innovative new ideas, the client evaluates them and then goes out to tender to find the lowest-cost supplier. In the case of the public sector, this is clearly not about ingratitude, but a simple legal imperative. From our perspective, we feel frustrated that we do not get the credit for the concept and then have to fight against latecomers, who may not understand the whole picture, for the right to execute on it. In the worst case, our competition then learns of our idea, and can apply it in competition with us in future bids.

Clearly, if this is the risk, a supplier is better off saving any new conceptual thinking for the next tender where rivals will not get the chance to respond. Since this will often be to a different client, the original client loses out altogether.

Simon Knowles of Computer Sciences Corporation (CSC) adds:

There is always a cost issue. CSC often proposes new, innovative approaches to problem-solving only to find that, after the client's initial enthusiasm, the clever stuff gets negotiated out of the deal to cut costs. Too often, at the final negotiation, innovative ideas are seen as a "nice to have".

CSC's response is to build a package of one-to-many knowledgebases. CSC Index is an IT analysis service that CSC can package in with its standard services, to give clients a source of original thinking. The fact that this operates as a cross-client service means that there is less risk of CSC's competitive advantage in any given account being compromised. CSC also runs a 'Leading Edge Forum' where it brings together key strategists to make technology forecasts and predictions. It also includes a web-based solution – the CSC Portal – that encourages collaborative work across the client base.

If innovation is a goal of an outsourcing project, clients must become more adept at putting in metrics for success around it and providing an environment where the outsourcer stands to gain from sharing its best ideas.

CHAPTER 45

STANDARD
TRANSACTIONAL
HIGHWAYS

‘Companies with sustainable competitive advantage integrate lots of activities within the business: their marketing, service, designs, customer support. All those things are consistent, interconnected and mutually reinforcing. ’ – Michael Porter[1]

Porter's thought leadership around value chains has had a huge impact on management practice. Software vendors were also quick to pick up on his concept of breaking down end-to-end processes into constituent parts. Just as such fine-tooth-comb analysis is vital for improving management processes, so it is key to added value in software design.

The first initiative was back-office automation, principally enterprise resource planning (ERP), which grew out of financials and manufacturing process automation to the point where it now touches almost every part of a company. HR was next, with PeopleSoft leading the market until the big ERP vendors (Oracle and SAP) started to compete.

Then, around five years ago, suppliers targeted the customer-facing front office. While there were already sales force automation technologies like ACT!, and helpdesk management tools aplenty, Siebel was an early pioneer of fully integrated front-office automation or, as it is now more commonly called, customer relationship management (CRM). Today, it is not uncommon for corporations to have systems costing hundreds of millions of dollars that run every element of their value chain.

But after the value chain has been defined and automated, the next logical step is to look at each step in the chain and ask:

- ☐ Is it core?

- ☐ Is it a competence? (It may add value to our clients, but others may be able to do it better.)

- ☐ Can it be operated discretely from the rest of the business?

172

---

[1] Michael Porter, *Competitive Advantage*, first edition The Free Press, 1985; new edition Simon & Schuster, 1998.

At a high level, the steps will be substantial – for example, logistics or accounts receivable are often outsourcing targets – but as the level of granularity increases, new options may open up.

Unisys's Peter Armstrong, a champion of the concept of standard transactional highways, explains that a standard process in most organizations is the setting up of new accounts. There will be many steps in this process, but one will usually be some form of credit-checking exercise. This standard transaction will be common to many businesses, and there is little value in every company building its own separate approach. New technologies like Java and Microsoft's .Net strategy are paving the way for companies to provide such standard transactions as tiny applications that can be delivered on an ASP basis and integrated seamlessly into the rest of a company's information systems. These internet technologies rely on standard interfaces, common agreed formats for data and powerful marketing initiatives from the big suppliers to press the other software developers to conform.

Ultimately, there could be a number of companies offering a credit-checking service and a free market for these tiny applications. The joy of technologies like .Net and Java is that the process of choosing which supplier to use can be automated, effectively creating a free market for every standard transactional service.

DUN & BRADSTREET

If this seems far fetched, consider Dun & Bradstreet (D&B). For over 100 years, it has been the arbiter of creditworthiness in the US and around the world. In fact the DUNS number (the unique company ID that appears on every one of D&B's 68 million company records) is the only common standard form of identity that covers virtually every trading body around the world. Many countries have standard numbers for their own companies; the UK Government, for example, issues every limited company with a unique ID from Companies House. This, however, does not cover partnerships, cooperatives or sole traders and therefore has limited value. D&B believes that its ubiquity gives the company a strong competitive advantage. Some countries, even in Western Europe, have a poor record in forcing companies to file financial accounts with the authorities – the penalty for failure can be lower than the cost of preparing the data.

According to Ian Green, head of third-party sales at D&B, the company is now committed to driving out 'business identification standards within transaction networks'. It regards verification as a component of the value chain – on both buy and sell sides. He says:

‘For the vast majority of companies, trading with a new customer or supplier means either a long delay while checks are carried out, or a credit card transaction. Credit cards are not an easy way for corporations to work. By bypassing normal processes they remove a level of due process. Relying on staff to use individual credit cards is bad for them and bad for the business too. D&B can take the role of an objective assessor in the middle. As companies move further into electronic trading, the inability to include new vendors or customers in the value chain without lengthy manual intervention is impractical and we see a role for ourselves in overcoming that problem.’

The D&B service comes in two components:

1 Identification. Is the organization real? Is it who it says it is?

2 Verification. Do people represent the company they claim to? Have they got the spending power?

D&B wants to embed the DUNS number into the standard transaction flow, effectively making it the only global standard identification number for companies. Already the US Government has adopted it as a standard for procurement processes. But while handing over intellectual property clearly represents a form of risk to a corporation like D&B, it also holds out the promise of putting the company in a very powerful position in the market. This has not escaped the notice of suppliers like Microsoft (with its UDDI services), nor the major global banks (which have formed a group called Identrus that has similar aims, though more focused on identification than verification). Whomever succeeds will be in a position to lead the market for this particular set of standard transactions.

CHAPTER 46

LEARNING
THE LESSONS
OF THE
OUTSOURCERS

In *Professional Services Firm 50*,[1] Tom Peters sets out to challenge every corporate white-collar worker to transform his or her department into a virtual professional services firm. Peters argues that by applying the processes, language and thinking of the services sector, departmental heads can inject more job satisfaction, more fun, more energy and more long-term chance of survival into their working lives. Throughout the book, Peters, in his customarily jolly style, lays out the principles that drive the services industry:

☐ Client portfolio management.

☐ Project-based working practices.

☐ Partnership-based agreements.

He also identifies business practices more commonly associated with independent businesses:

☐ A uniquely identified vision and value set.

☐ A culture which is discrete from the rest of the corporation.

☐ Talent development.

☐ Brand identity.

Once the trauma of a switch-over has passed, outsourced staff often comment on the cultural aspects of their change of employer. Many talk of the satisfaction to be gained from working in a team with a clear identity, where their work feels relevant to the business (rather than peripheral or, worse, an overhead). In fact, outsourcers regard this cultural shift as the key to driving new efficiencies in working practice, especially in a BPO context. In his book, Peters effectively argues that the business can gain most of the cultural benefits of outsourcing without involving any third parties at all.

[1] Tom Peters, *Professional Services Firm 50*, Alfred A Knopf, 1999.

Guy Warren, VP for service delivery at Unisys, agrees:

> (We see two distinct domains of outsourcing benefits, especially in IT outsourcing – those which are unique to the outsourcing process and those that can be applied to in-house teams with dramatic success.)

Benefits that outsourcing brings include:

☐ IT refreshment.

☐ Best practice process optimization – new approaches that come from external experiences.

☐ Economies of scale.

☐ Ability to leverage larger organization's assets and infrastructure.

☐ Capital requirements.

☐ Management focus.

Benefits outsourcing brings that can be developed in-house:

☐ Customer-supplier model.

☐ Metrics that are meaningful to the business.

☐ 'Core competence' attitude.

The customer-supplier model means a shift in thinking from user to customer. Once users, or the departments in which they work, are considered as and treated like customers, it becomes far easier to be objective about the quality of service and the reasonableness of demands.

Many IT operations are loathe to introduce independent benchmarking. Some prefer to 'wait until we get it right'; others fear that benchmarking will open them up to easy comparison with third parties and so precipitate outsourcing. We find that, where IT operations are not benchmarked, they are constantly measured only against perfection. Where the IT operation has agreed mutually acceptable metrics for success with its internal clients, satisfaction levels climb. For example, if an IT department has no metrics for success, it may have an e-mail system that operates at 98 per cent availability and causes howls of complaints. With metrics in place, the CIO can approach the business and offer to improve availability to 99.5 per cent, but at a cost of $750,000. The business can then work with the CIO to decide whether the extra availability is really that important. Whatever the decision, internal customers' satisfaction will rise as it is they who have made the choice about what is important to them.

Industry benchmarking does invite comparison, but that may not be a bad thing – surely it is better to be compared against a third party based on metrics that you control, than on the basis of non-empirical data and perceived service quality. Indeed, an IT department that is effectively measured against agreed SLAs is far less likely to be outsourced, or – if it is – it is likely that the IT management will be a key part of the decision process.

But it is not just IT that can learn the lessons of outsourcing. The core competence attitude ('what we do is important') can be created by any manager, in any operational department, who is willing to invest the time and energy.

CHAPTER 47

HOW FAR CAN OUTSOURCING REALLY GO?

As companies look to shift from functionally managed services to the complete outsourcing of business processes, suddenly everything looks like a possible outsourcing target. Where does it end?

Martin Dines is head of IT outsourcing for Unisys EMEA. He says:

❛ As BPO contracts become ever more ambitious in scope, so the level of risk increases for both outsourcer and client. In the case of UISL [*see case study, Chapter 17*], the new venture is probably taking on around 85 per cent of the client's total workload. This service therefore has implications for the company's reputation, the Data Protection Act and Abbey Life's customer relationships, as well as for Lloyds TSB, the parent company. The SLA is therefore extremely sophisticated and we have a very strong governance process in place under a very strong leader. It is hard to see how much more risk can safely be built into a contract and legislated for in a service level agreement. There comes a point where the line between outsourcing and merger or acquisition becomes blurred. ❜

Perhaps the real bottleneck in the development of the outsourcing market is not the technology, or even the possibilities. It may just be the mundane question of how quickly new approaches can be developed for measuring, minimizing and legislating for risk.

SUMMARY

1 Bandwidth will be sufficient for large systems suppliers to build and house hardware outside the G7 community, and allow customers to connect remotely.

2 Traditional large, in-house IT departments will die out as staff recruitment becomes ever more difficult and the cost of maintaining mainframe systems in-house becomes unviable.

3 Technology commoditization will give outsourcers even more power to secure good deals with hardware suppliers.

4 If the ASP model takes off, there will be a need for 'ASP aggregators' to act as single points of delivery for multiple ASP services.

5 Expect further consolidation in the FM sector, as specialist suppliers realize that they must offer a full range of services if they are to grow margins.

6 In a global market, innovation will become increasingly vital to success. If clients are to capitalize on outsourcers' thought leadership skills, they must put in specific metrics and gain-share provisions to encourage innovative idea generation.

7 Standard transactional highways, built on technologies such as .Net and Java, will grow to the point where organizations are able to buy in and seamlessly integrate highly granular, non-core services, delivered via the internet.

8 In-house operational departments (such as IT and HR) will apply the lessons of the outsourcers and begin to operate on a similar, customer-supplier basis, with agreed metrics in place and an attitude of core competence.

9 How far outsourcing goes may ultimately depend on how quickly we develop new approaches to measure, minimize and legislate for risk.

BIBLIOGRAPHY

Byron Auguste, Yvonne Hao, Marc Singer and Michael Wiegand, 'The Other Side of Outsourcing' in *McKinsey Quarterly*, 2002 Number 1

Jeremy Bigwood, 'DynCorp in Colombia: Outsourcing the Drug War' in CorpWatch report, 23 May 2000, www.corpwatch.org

Stephen Covey, *The 7 Habits of Highly Effective People*, Simon & Schuster, 1989

Paul De La Garza and David Adams, 'Military Aid . . . From The Private Sector' in *St Petersburg Times*, 3 December 2000

Charles Drayson, 'Don't Leave it All to the Lawyers', in *Computer Weekly*, 13 December 2001

Dun & Bradstreet, 'Barometer of Global Outsourcing', 2000

Liam Fahey, *Outwitting, Outmanoeuvring and Outperforming Competitors*, John Wiley & Sons, 1998

Tom Field, 'How to Adopt Your Offshore Strategy to an Insecure World', in *CIO Magazine*, 1 January 2002

Pimm Fox, 'CRM Nightmare Will Go Away', in *ComputerWorld*, 7 December 2001

Larry Greenemeier, 'Companies Reconsider Offshore Outsourcing', in *InformationWeek*, 10 December 2001

Naomi Klein, *No Logo*, Flamingo, 2001

Tom Peters, *Professional Services Firm 50*, Alfred A Knopf, 1999

The Tom Peters Seminar – Crazy Times Call for Crazy Organisations, Macmillan, 1994

Michael Porter, *Competitive Advantage*, first edition The Free Press, 1985; new edition Simon & Schuster, 1998

Morgan Chambers and *CW360, Outsourcing in the FTSE 100 – The Definitive Study*, 2001

CK Prahalad and Gary Hamel, 'The Core Competence of the Corporation', originally published in *Harvard Business Review*, 1990; also features in the collection *Competence-Based Competition*, edited by Gary Hamel and Amie Heene, John Wiley & Sons, 1994

David Shearer, 'Privatising Protection' in *World Today*, August/September 2001, www.riia.org/wt.html

Paul A Strassman, *Transforming IT Costs Into Profits*, Butler Group report, May 2001

Patrick Thibodean, 'Federal Government Eyes More Outsourcing' in *ComputerWorld*, 18 April 2001

Charles Wang, *Techno Vision*, McGraw-Hill, 1994

APPENDIX

RESEARCH DATA

The content of this book is based on input from some of the smartest, best-informed people in the outsourcing industry. In assembling the overviews and advice, I have tried to balance end-user, supplier and independent consultant viewpoints to build an even-handed perspective on the pros and cons, benefits and risks of outsourcing.

TELEPHONE RESEARCH INTERVIEWS

However, in order to further ensure a completely balanced view, Unisys, sponsor of the book, also ran a telephone research program. In total, 269 executives (mostly finance directors) were approached and a 40 per cent response was achieved, with the majority of input coming from Switzerland, The Netherlands and the UK. France was the least willing to participate, with just one out of 19 contacts agreeing to be interviewed.

The split of responding interviewees was as follows:

COUNTRY	RESPONSE PERCENTAGE
Belgium	2
France	1
Germany	8
The Netherlands	19
Switzerland	14
UK	55

TABLE A1: Percentage split of countries who responded to the interview

What do they outsource?

Of the 106 respondents, nearly half had not outsourced anything at all. Of the remainder, the split is shown in Figure A1.

Across this very small sample, German organizations were the most prolific outsourcers with 89 per cent of respondents identifying projects they had undertaken, compared with just 13 per cent of Swiss respondents.

Interestingly, when asked whether they outsource business processes, only one of the 16 positive responses came from outside the UK, suggesting that the UK market is more open to BPO than others. This would tend to support the assumptions made in Part 4, that the UK is ahead on this approach to service delivery.

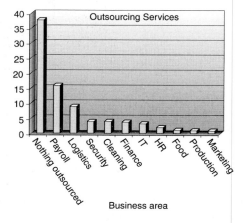

FIGURE A1: Aspects of business outsourced

Why outsource?

The findings here match those of most other recent surveys, with a heavy focus on cost savings (see Figure A2). There was no significant variation in motives among the countries.

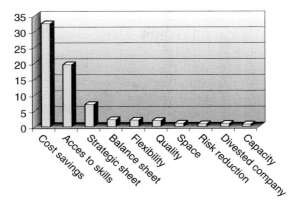

FIGURE A2: Reasons to outsource

The benefits achieved

Next, participants that had outsourced were asked with which areas they were most satisfied (Figure A3).

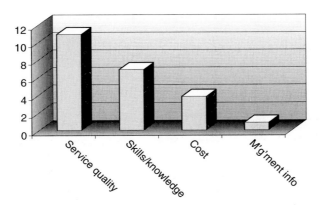

FIGURE A3: Source of greatest satisfaction

Interestingly, despite the fact that the vast majority outsourced with a view to saving money, cost savings were only cited as the primary benefit by four respondents. The strongest positive response was around service quality. This chimes with the comments made by most of the people interviewed in the book that, while cost is the primary driver for kicking off an outsourcing engagement, there is almost always an implicit expectation of service quality improvement.

Time to establish operational standards

Most people I interviewed in researching this book warned that it takes longer than many people expect to achieve a service running on all cylinders. In the survey we asked people how long it took to reach a smooth level of service (Figure A4 overleaf).

183

Those stating 12 months or longer were, by and large, unhappy with the service and I suspect that the issue here is not to do with ramp-up, but is at an altogether deeper level.

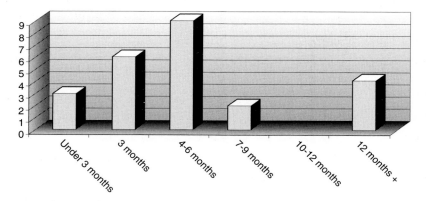

FIGURE A4: Time to achieve smooth running

Most respondents took an average of three to four months to get the service running to their satisfaction, which supports the anecdotal evidence in the rest of the book.

Why decide against outsourcing?

We asked companies who had considered outsourcing and decided not to go ahead, what drove this decision.

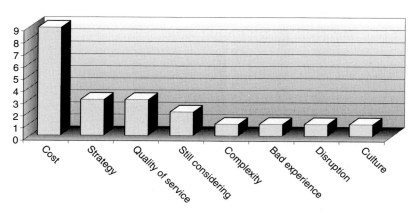

FIGURE A5: Reasons not to outsource

ADVICE

What did our sample survey yield in the way of advice for potential outsourcing clients? We started by asking for general advice for potential clients. The responses broke down into the following categories:

Be prepared

☐ 'Talk to someone who has done it and understands exactly what is and is not covered.'

☐ 'Enter into negotiations after thorough preparation.'

☐ 'Go into the outsourcing process well prepared. Make sure that you and the outsourcing partner agree all the arrangements, and define all parameters exactly.'

Establish your own expectations

☐ 'Be absolutely clear about what it is you expect and always define/break down the small print.'

☐ 'Make sure the contract is what you want and understand the management relationship.'

☐ 'Plan well.'

☐ 'Take care when listening to what you are told by sales reps! They invariably only deliver 90 per cent of what the salesperson says.'

☐ 'Be specific as to what you are looking to outsource and your requirements.'

☐ 'Know what you want to achieve through outsourcing.'

Do not rush into outsourcing

☐ 'Look at it carefully.'

☐ 'Take time to consider all options.'

☐ 'Weigh up the risks.'

Choose the partner carefully

☐ 'Be sure that your company is organized enough for the change and new structure.'

☐ 'Pick the right company for you. Make sure that they are fully aware of the changes it will cause in the company.'

☐ 'Always get two or three alternatives/opinions before making a final decision.'

☐ 'Pick supplier wisely and do not be the first.'

☐ 'Focus on quality of service.'

Spend time on contractual issues

☐ 'Make sure they review the contract thoroughly first.'

☐ 'Check and understand the contract fully and make sure you know the service you will be getting.'

Be certain of the outsourcer's capability

☐ 'Make sure that the outsourcing partner has intensive know-how in the specialist areas that they represent your firm in.'

☐ 'Carefully consider the whole process and verify the competence of your potential outsourcing partner.'

☐ 'Make sure that the outsourcing partner can offer you the most relevant technological expertise.'